THE LEADER'S GUIDE TO
LATERAL THINKING SKILLS

THIRD EDITION

THE LEADER'S GUIDE TO
LATERAL THINKING SKILLS

Unlock the creativity and innovation in you and your team

PAUL SLOANE

KoganPage

First published in Great Britain and the United States in 2003 by Kogan Page Limited
Third edition published 2017

2nd Floor, 45 Gee Street	c/o Martin P Hill Consulting	4737/23 Ansari Road
London	122 W 27th St, 10th Floor	Daryaganj
EC1V 3RS	New York, NY 10001	New Delhi 110002
United Kingdom	USA	India

www.koganpage.com

© Paul Sloane, 2017

The right of Paul Sloane to be identified as the author of this work has been asserted by him in accordance with the Copyright, Designs and Patents Act 1988.

ISBN   978 0 7494 8102 5
E-ISBN   978 0 7494 8103 2

British Library Cataloguing-in-Publication Data

A CIP record for this book is available from the British Library.

Library of Congress Cataloging-in-Publication Data
Names: Sloane, Paul, 1950- author. | Sloane, Paul, 1950- The innovative
   leader.
Title: The leader's guide to lateral thinking skills : unlock the creativity
   and innovation in you and your team / Paul Sloane.
Other titles: Lateral thinking skills
Description: 3rd Edition. | New York, NY : Kogan Page Ltd, [2017] | Revised
   edition of the author's The leader's guide to skills, 2006. | Includes
   bibliographical references and index.
Identifiers: LCCN 2017022348 (print) | LCCN 2017021056 (ebook) | ISBN
   9780749481032 (ebook) | ISBN 9780749481025 (pbk.) | ISBN 9780749481032
   (eISBN)
Subjects: LCSH: Creative ability in business. | Lateral thinking. |
   Management.
Classification: LCC HD53 (print) | LCC HD53 .S57 2017 (ebook) | DDC
   658.4/0714–dc23
LC record available at https://lccn.loc.gov/2017021056

Typeset by Integra Software Services, Pondicherry
Print production managed by Jellyfish
Printed and bound by CPI Group (UK) Ltd, Croydon, CR0 4YY

This work is dedicated to my wife, Ann, and daughters, Jacqueline, Valentina and Hannah, whose understanding and support are much appreciated.

CONTENTS

ACKNOWLEDGEMENTS

I would like to thank the following people for their help and inspiration with this book: Roger Jeynes, Bill Penn, Ajaz Ahmed, Brian McBride, Andrew Needham and Ian Gander. I would also like to recognize the lessons learnt in working with clients including AKQA, ARM, BT, Bayer, Equant, IBM, MathSoft, Nike, Reckitt Benckiser, Shell, Swarovski, Vodafone and others.

The lateral thinking puzzles are mostly drawn from the series of books by Paul Sloane and Des MacHale published by Sterling Publishing of New York.

Introduction

Out there is an entrepreneur who is forging a bullet with your company's name on it. You've got one option now – to shoot first. You've got to out-innovate the innovators.
GARY HAMEL

Many CEOs, directors and senior managers in business today are focused on improving efficiency, making things work better and delivering better customer service. They are working extremely hard and think they are doing a good job. They are not. This is because incremental improvement in the existing business is not enough. In addition to improving current operations, leaders must spend time looking for entirely new ways to meet customer needs. They should select and implement different and better ways of meeting the corporate goals. In addition to running today's business, they should be starting bold new initiatives – some of which will fail and some of which will succeed. Above all, they must encourage and empower their people to take a creative and entrepreneurial approach to exploit new opportunities.

Directors constantly strive to deliver increased shareholder value by improving cash flow through efficiencies of scale and cost reductions. But there are strict limits to how many cost savings you can make. In a global economy, your competitors in lower-cost countries can beat you at that game. The best way to create value is to innovate your way ahead of the competition in order to create temporary monopolies where yours is the only show in town. You can do this by harnessing the creative power of your greatest asset, your people. The goal is to turn them into opportunistic entrepreneurs who are constantly looking for new ways of doing business.

This is where lateral thinking comes in. Lateral thinking means approaching business challenges from new directions in order to conceive radical and better solutions. The key is for the leader to encourage and develop lateral thinking skills in his or her team. How can you make all your staff into creative entrepreneurs? How can you energize people to see problems not as obstacles to success but as opportunities for innovation? How can you spur couch potatoes on to become intrepid explorers? What practical techniques can you use in your everyday work to lead by example, to inspire and to motivate people around you to become more creative? The goal of this book is to give you the lateral tools and techniques to create a climate of creativity and to transform your organization into a powerhouse of innovation. That is the destination.

Richard Branson of Virgin Group, Elon Musk of Tesla Motors and SpaceX, Jeff Bezos of Amazon and Travis Kalanick of Uber are renowned for encouraging and welcoming ideas from their employees – and for acting quickly on them.

First, we will explore what makes a lateral leader, the kind of person who can create a climate of creativity by inspiring people to have the confidence to take risks, and who can then develop their skills in creative techniques. We will see how these leaders paint a vision for the organization, communicate it and derive goals and objectives from the vision. They spend enormous effort on the culture of the business in order to make it open, questioning and receptive to new ideas. We will explain the principles and rules for creativity that the lateral leader uses and embodies, and look at practical exercises for implementing these principles. We will examine the structures and policies to put in place in order to make innovation a process that runs through the organization like blood through the veins. We will draw on examples throughout of how people in all walks of life have made innovation a reality by applying these rules, principles and processes. And to challenge your creative problem-solving skills, we will set some of the examples as lateral thinking puzzles for you to solve.

The key elements of creating a truly innovative and entrepreneurial organization can be summarized in the following nine steps:

1 Paint an inspiring vision.

2 Build an open, receptive, questioning culture.

3 Empower people at all levels.

4 Set goals, deadlines and measurements for innovation.

5 Use creativity techniques to generate a large number of ideas.

6 Review, combine, filter and select ideas.

7 Prototype the promising proposals.

8 Welcome failure and manage risk.

9 Analyse results and roll out the successful projects.

01
The need for innovation

Every organization has to prepare for the abandonment of everything it does.
PETER DRUCKER

The challenge of change

Sometimes the situation you are in is so tough that you just cannot work your way out of the problem. You have to think your way out of the problem. But most organizations are resistant to rapid and discontinuous change. They operate as they have operated in the past. It is as though they learnt to walk from A to B and now they are finding it tough to walk from B to C. So they try to walk faster. They work harder and try to improve efficiency but they are still not getting there. Instead of working harder they should be working smarter – and differently. There is a better way of getting from B to C than by walking; maybe it is cycling or riding or driving or taking a helicopter. There is a better way of reaching your organization's goals, and if you look hard enough you will find it. But you cannot look in a new direction if you are staring hard in the one direction in which your business is focused.

Many organizations are stuck in their standard mode of operation.

They strive to make the existing model work better and don't spend time looking for a better model, a better way of doing things. As the management guru Gary Hamel puts it: 'Most companies are built for continuous improvement, rather than for discontinuous innovation. They know how to get better, but they don't know how to get different.'

'Only the paranoid will survive,' said Andy Grove, Chairman of Intel, the company that dominates the PC processor business. You have to be paranoid about improving the goods and services that you offer your clients, because if you don't somebody else will. Intel's philosophy is to cannibalize its own business by constantly bringing out better processors to replace the ones that are already market leaders. Grove knows that resting on your laurels is a sure way to slide into complacency and defeat at the hands of an innovative competitor.

Another company that exemplifies this approach is Gillette, part of Procter & Gamble, which has a policy of making its own products obsolete. They deliberately launch razors with more blades or better features in order to displace their own market-leading products. They do not stand still long enough to give competitors a way in. Like Intel, every time Gillette launches a new product it is already working on the product that will replace it. Successful companies and their leaders do not allow success to blunt the drive for innovation, a never-ending race to overtake themselves.

Managers in every organization have a responsibility for initiating and directing change in addition to their regular objectives. Everyone has the shared responsibility of changing the organization to make it better equipped to meet the needs of its customers, and of keeping finding innovative ways to deliver its products or services. Just doing better what you do today is not enough.

We tend to think that it is just the boffins in research and development who should dream up new products, and the VP of marketing who has to create fresh ways of promoting the products, but the reality is that everyone has the opportunity and duty to be creative. The VP of sales has to figure out new approaches to reach customers and motivate their channel partners. The HR director has to find creative ways to attract and retain staff. The CFO has to find innovative processes to take cost out of the supply chain while increasing quality and service. The CIO has to find new ways to deliver projects on time and make them easy enough for people to understand and use.

The competition is fierce. In the wild market economy of today it is increasingly difficult to differentiate yourself. When the consumer has a wealth of choice, what were previously good products become commodities. The challenge is to think of new and better ways to solve the needs of the customer. To be truly competitive you have to be different and that means thinking laterally and innovating.

To do this in today's world requires a different style of leadership: lateral leadership. The conventional leader is fine when what is needed is command and control of a well-defined process. But for rapid and discontinuous change, the lateral leader is better equipped. He or she focuses on developing the skills of the team in innovation, creativity, risk taking and entrepreneurial endeavour. The lateral leader manages change by initiating it.

In the late 1970s, the Swiss watch industry faced extinction. Fierce competition from the Japanese with mass production of cheap but good-quality electronic products was driving major Swiss brands like Omega, Longines and Tissot out of business. Nicholas Hayek devised a plan involving the merger of two of the largest Swiss watch manufacturers, ASUAG and SSIH, in order to form a new company with a different approach to watch design: to create a low-cost, high-tech, artistic and emotional watch – the Swatch. Within five years the new company was the largest watchmaker in the world. Hayek became its chairman. Swatch rewrote the rules of the watch industry by making watches that were fun, fashionable and collectable.

Change, creativity and innovation

Change involves moving from one condition to another, but change is not necessarily innovation. A church that becomes a sports gym club has undertaken a radical change but it has not innovated. There are plenty of other gym clubs. But a church that combines prayer meetings with aerobic exercise classes has innovated. Innovation is bringing something new into existence. Similarly, a company that fires half its workforce in order to cut costs has undertaken a major change. But a company that finds a fundamentally new way to reach and serve its customers has innovated.

To change:	To alter, make different, move from one state to another.
Creativity:	The state or quality of being creative. The ability to create.
Innovation:	The act of introducing something new, a thing that is introduced as a novelty.
Lateral thinking:	Thinking that seeks new ways of looking at a problem rather than proceeding by logical steps.

A person or organization that is creative is not necessarily innovative. Creativity is the ability or talent to create. It is about generating ideas. Innovation is the implementation of the new. Innovation means taking creative ideas and making them real, implementing them. Innovation is not just releasing new products. It also encompasses implementing new business processes, fresh ways of doing things, radical alliances, new routes to market and business strategies.

Creativity must be viewed as a means to an end and not an end in itself. The end is innovation – the realization of an idea. Uncontrolled creativity without any discipline or process of innovation is at best distracting and at worst harmful to the organization. Creativity needs to be focused on the corporate goals and must serve as a funnel into the innovation process. Innovation means taking the most promising ideas and testing them for real. Not all will succeed; many will fail. Despite some failures along the way, the people in a truly innovative organization are always looking for new and entrepreneurial ways of achieving their goals.

Lateral thinking

Creative thinking is a generic term to describe any approach that is new. Lateral thinking is a term created by Edward de Bono to describe a set of approaches and techniques designed to find radically new approaches to problems – to come at them from the side rather than the front.

In the early part of the 20th century, all shops were places where the assistant served the customer. The customer would come to the counter and the assistant would fetch the items that the customer required. In the 1920s, a man called Michael Cullen took a different view. He asked the question, 'What would happen if we turned the shop around and let the customer help themselves to the goods they wanted and then they paid at the end?' There were doubtless many who objected to this notion. 'Customers want service, they do not want to do all the work themselves'; 'All the goods will have to be priced'; 'People will get confused if there is no assistant to help them'; 'What, you mean let people wander round the back of the store?'; and so on. But Cullen persisted and created the world's first supermarket, the King Kullen store in New Jersey.

What a simple idea – but what a powerful one. The mere notion of letting the customer serve themselves has transformed not only our shops but our town layouts – with the old fashioned main street full of small shops replaced by large self-service superstores.

Michael Cullen did some lateral thinking. He showed lateral leadership by conceiving an entirely new way of serving customers and then driving his idea through to completion. The difference between creative thinking and lateral thinking is the difference between introducing any kind of new shop and introducing a new approach to shopping entirely – the supermarket.

This book will show how lateral leaders use creative and lateral thinking techniques to transform their organization into a hotbed of entrepreneurial spirit brimming with new ideas. Lateral leaders inspire and coach their teams to reach the goal of becoming a truly creative force and thereby to achieve breakthrough solutions they never thought possible.

Lateral thinking puzzles

Lateral thinking puzzles are problems where you have to think differently and use fresh approaches to solve the problem. They are generally used as exercises in questioning techniques and imaginative problem solving. There is a fuller description in Appendix 1 (Exercise N). You will encounter some as you go through this book as a little light relief and examples of creative problem solving. They encourage you to challenge your assumptions, to ask questions and to come at the problem from fresh directions. They are best played as a team game, as explained in the Appendix. Can you figure out the lateral solutions to the problems? The answers are given at the end of the book.

THE SUBWAY PROBLEM

A large city in the United States had a problem with thefts of light bulbs from its subway system. Thieves would unscrew the light bulbs, leading to cost and security issues. The engineer who was given this challenge could not alter the location of the light bulbs, and he had very little budget to work with, but he came up with a very lateral solution. What was it?

02
Characteristics of the lateral leader

In periods where there is no leadership, society stands still. Progress occurs when courageous, skilful leaders seize the opportunity to change things for the better.

HARRY S TRUMAN

The conventional leader is easily recognized as a goal-oriented, decisive person who is well suited to a structured environment such as a mature corporation, government department or the military. Lateral leaders, on the other hand, adopt a different approach to reaching goals – they are much more focused on the creativity and innovation of the team. The lateral leader is often found in small, fast-moving high-tech companies that have collegial and intellectual environments.

The conventional leader is focused on action, results, efficiency and process improvement. The lateral leader is focused on inspiring the team to find new and better ways of doing things. In this chapter we will contrast the style and approach of the two types of leader.

Successful leaders combine the qualities of the conventional leader and the lateral leader. They know when to focus on efficiency and results and when to focus on vision, coaching and inspiration. But most managers are in the left-hand, conventional column. They are ingrained with analysis, results, efficiency, command and control. As they rise through the organization they need to take on more of the right-hand, lateral column. They need to loosen some of their grip on analysis and detail. They must delegate more and focus on empowering the team to find innovative ways of making the vision a reality.

There is a real risk that potential leaders who start out with great creative energy and rise through an organization become more institutionalized and lose their innovative zest. Businesses and institutions that promote people who conform to their corporate standards will most likely end up with efficient and hard-working leaders who operate inside a corporate comfort zone. Unfortunately, that is nowhere near enough. Today's president, CEO or managing director needs to be a disruptive influence with the imagination, vision and courage to lead the organization into new and dangerous territory. The leader must be an entrepreneurial driver who can inspire the team to boldly venture into uncharted lands. This requires conventional and lateral leadership skills.

Is a lateral leader born or made? Can a conventional manager acquire the traits of the lateral leader? Can creativity be engendered in everyone or are there just a few people who naturally have the creative spark inside them? The answer is that while some people are naturally better leaders or more creative, everyone has creative abilities within them. Everyone can learn techniques that will lead them to generate more and better ideas. Every manager who aspires to a senior position can learn and apply the traits and principles of the lateral leader.

VANDAL SCANDAL

The authorities in Athens were very concerned that tourists sometimes hacked pieces from the ancient columns of the Parthenon building. The practice was illegal but some people were determined to take away souvenirs. How did the authorities stop this practice?

Conventional leaders	Lateral leaders
Lead from the front	Lead from alongside
Direct	Inspire
Use conventional methods and seek to improve effectiveness and efficiency	Develop new methods and seek to change the rules, change partners or change the approach to the problem
Think they know best (and often do)	Harness the abilities of others
Have a strong sense of direction and purpose	Have a vision and use it to inspire others

Conventional leaders	Lateral leaders
Spend more time on improving day-to-day operational matters than on strategic issues	Spend more time on finding new strategic initiatives and partners than on solving operational or day-to-day matters
Give directions and orders	Ask questions, solicit suggestions, delegate
Look for greater efficiency, more productivity, faster development, more aggressive sales and marketing	Look for new ways to do things, new approaches to the customer, new solutions, new partnerships
Treat staff as subordinates	Treat staff as colleagues
Are decisive, often without prior consultation	Solicit views and inputs before making decisions
Use analytical, critical, logical thinking	Use lateral thinking
Build an effective team of managers who can execute policy and implement plans	Build a team of creative, entrepreneurial individuals
Focus on actions and results	Focus on direction and innovation to achieve results
Communicate through memos and e-mail	Communicate through open discussion
Instruct	Empower
Hire based on experience, proven track record and qualifications	Hire based on talent, potential and creativity
Discourage dissent	Encourage constructive dissent
Cherish results first, people second	Cherish ideas, innovation and people
Promote themselves as leaders and figureheads with the press, customers and the outside world	Share exposure and prestige with the team
Encourage action, activity, work	Encourage ideas, innovation, fun
Reward performance and results	Reward creativity and risk taking
Are numbers oriented and analytical	Are ideas oriented, analytical and intuitive
See technology as a means to do things better, faster, cheaper	See technology as a means to do things entirely differently
Overrule ideas and initiatives they see as flawed or wrong	Encourage all initiative and often implement ideas or suggestions over which they have doubts
Look for ideas from their own experience	Look for ideas from anywhere!

SOURCE based on Sloane (1999)

03
The innovation test

The temptation in business is always to feed yesterday and to starve tomorrow.
PETER DRUCKER

Before we look at how to develop skills in innovation, creativity and lateral thinking, let's take stock to see how innovative your organization is right now. To check your innovation level try answering these questions about your organization:

Question	Strongly disagree	Moderately disagree	Moderately agree	Strongly agree
Score	1	2	3	4
1 Everyone understands the overall goals and direction of the organization				
2 Fresh ideas are encouraged and tried out				
3 We often have brainstorming or other creative workshops				
4 People are trained in creativity and innovation				
5 People are praised and rewarded for being creative				

Question	Strongly disagree	Moderately disagree	Moderately agree	Strongly agree
6 We deliberately copy and adapt good ideas from outside our field				
7 We appoint teams from different departments to solve specific problems				
8 When we are looking to solve a problem we generate a lot of ideas before choosing one or two to try				
9 We often build prototypes or pilots to test a new idea rapidly before a production version				
10 To solve a problem in one department we would call for ideas and help from other departments				
11 We identify current products and processes that are due for retirement and replacement				
12 We set goals for innovation, including the introduction of new products and processes				
13 We have a 'not invented here' attitude to ideas from outside				

Question	Strongly disagree	Moderately disagree	Moderately agree	Strongly agree
14 People are scared to take too many risks for fear of failure				
15 The boss's ideas carry the greatest weight				
16 We are too busy fixing today's problems to spend much time thinking about the future				
17 New ideas stand little chance of being carried out if they are not in the budget				

The first twelve questions carry positive scores and the last five questions carry negative scores. So add together your scores for questions 1 to 12 and then subtract your scores for questions 13 to 17. Your overall total is your innovation index. How did you do?

Over 33: You are working in a very enlightened organization where innovation and communication levels are high.

25 to 32: There is a good atmosphere for innovation and new ideas are welcomed but there is still scope for improvement.

18 to 24: You are a little better than average but there is a long way to go to reach the innovation levels of the best organizations.

11 to 17: You are below average and need to work on improving your climate for innovation and creative problem solving.

5 to 10: Significant barriers exist to your organization coping with change or adapting to new conditions. This could be dangerous and needs a major programme to address it.

4 or below: You have deep-seated resistance to change and new ideas are not encouraged or rewarded. The culture of your organization needs a major long-term programme of change if it is to survive.

A supplementary question is, 'What new things have you done in the past year that your competitors would have liked to have done?' Or to put it another way, 'What innovations have you implemented that have had positive impacts on customers?' These are the acid tests of innovation. Innovative organizations lead. They do things that impress clients and other people in their industry. If you cannot think of such examples or find that they are all very small, incremental things, then chances are that yours is not an innovative organization.

Applying the principles in this book will raise your innovation index. Organizing and structuring for innovation is something that every management team can undertake once it is seen as a priority. Innovation is something that can be developed, encouraged and managed. Transforming a corporate culture that is resistant to change into one which welcomes and initiates it is one of the toughest of management challenges. But it is one that has to be faced.

SHOE SHOP SHUFFLE

In a small town there are four shoe shops of about the same size and each carries a similar line of shoes. Yet one shop loses three times as many shoes to theft as each of the other shops. Why is this and how did they fix the problem?

04
Laying the foundations for change

Inaction is not an option.
GEORGE W BUSH

Recognizing the need for change

Lateral leaders are focused on change, but around them there are many who are quite happy with the current state of affairs. The first challenges that the leader faces are how to communicate the need for change, and how to secure the buy-in of the people in the organization. 'Inaction is not an option' is a mantra that has to be taken up in organizations where change is needed but the need for change is not fully recognized.

The natural tendency for business managers is to focus on improving efficiency and refining the current processes because it is clear that 'we can do things better'. Improving efficiency is important but it is not enough. If you were making horse-drawn carriages then it did not matter how much you improved efficiency, because automobiles were going to put you out of business. If you were making gas lamps and you focused on better production, it did not help because electric lights were going to make your lamps obsolete. If you were making LP records then it did not matter how much time you spent on quality improvement programmes because CDs were going to wipe you out. And if you were making typewriters then it did not help however much you improved the mechanical operations because electronic word processors were going to destroy your business. The message is that innovation beats efficiency. You have to improve what you are doing but you also have to find entirely new and better ways to do it.

The leader has to communicate the message that doing what we do now, only better, is not enough. If you do what you always did then you will get what you always got. You have to do something different to get different results. You have to do something significantly smarter to get significantly better results.

Painting the vision

The lateral leader invests in painting a picture of where the organization is headed. There is plenty of hype talked about 'vision', and it is easy to become sceptical about it, but a vision is important. During the dark days of the Second World War, when Britain stood alone against the power of Nazi Germany, Winston Churchill never wavered from his vision – a vision of victory. He spoke in flowing terms about the 'sunlit uplands' which would be the reward for the hardships currently being endured. He inspired the nation at a very difficult time and made people believe that victory was possible.

General Electric Company's (GE) mission is to 'build, move, power, and cure the world'.

The Ford Motor Company's vision is: 'People working together as a lean, global enterprise to make people's lives better through automotive and mobility leadership.'

GlaxoSmithKline's (GSK) mission statement is 'to help people do more, feel better, live longer'.

Vision statements should be short and inspiring. They should avoid vague and woolly clichés about outstanding customer service. The vision should not be restricted to today's type of business. It must set a goal that gives employees enormous freedom in finding ways to achieve it. The pharmaceutical giant GlaxoSmithKline does not define its mission in mundane terms of drugs or medicines or markets, but in inspirational terms of helping people do more, feel better and live longer.

Figure 4.1 The four elements of the vision

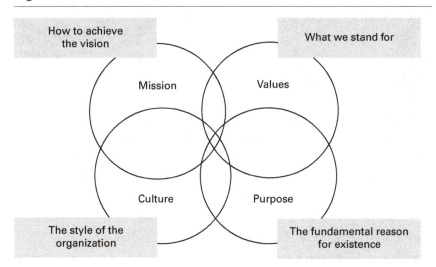

To construct a corporate vision you need to consider four components. These are your purpose, your mission, your culture and your values. The purpose is the fundamental reason for the existence of the organization. The mission expresses the purpose as a strategic goal. The culture defines the style of the organization – how it does things. The values are the beliefs of the organization – what it stands for. These four elements underpin the vision, which is an inspiring statement of the destination of the company. It is a challenging but achievable dream. The vision and the mission are often similar, and some organizations have just the one statement here rather than two. For more on how to construct a vision, see Chapter 23, the lateral leadership course.

The vision does not have to be defined in detail. However, it must be recognizable as something ambitious but achievable for the enterprise. When in 1961 President Kennedy famously set out the goal of a moon landing he did it with one simple sentence: 'I believe that this nation should commit itself to landing a man on the moon and returning him safely to Earth before this decade is out.' The vision was clear. The timescale was set. The challenge was thrown down. It was accepted and accomplished. Painting a scene that is desirable, challenging and believable is the task of the lateral leader. If you can do this then there are three big gains for the organization.

First, people share a common goal and have a sense of embarking on a journey or adventure together. This means they are more willing to accept the changes, challenges and difficulties that any journey can entail.

Second, it means that more responsibility can be delegated. Staff can be empowered and given more control over their work. Because they know the goal and direction in which they are headed, they can be trusted to steer their own raft and to figure out the best way of getting there.

Third, people will be more creative and contribute more ideas if they know that there are unsolved challenges that lie ahead. They have bought into the adventure so they are more ready to find routes over and around the obstacles on the way.

The vision is the platform on which the corporate plans are built. From the vision flow the corporate key values and messages, and the strategic goals – the ways in which over the long term the vision will be achieved. The strategic goals lead to the tactical objectives and targets that operate in the short and medium term. From these flow the departmental and individual objectives that direct and motivate all the staff. If people understand the process of how their departmental goals derive from the corporate vision and strategic objectives then they can set their own individual objectives. Of course, this is part of a dialogue with their team leaders.

The other important outcome that can be derived from the vision and the strategic goals is the innovation objective. This expresses the specific targets in terms of new products, processes, partnerships, etc. which the organization needs to support its goals. Examples of innovation objectives for the next two years might be:

- Forty per cent of product revenues in year two from new product lines (ie not existing today).
- Two ventures in new markets.
- New supply chain processes to halve inventory and cut supply costs by 20 per cent.
- Three new strategic partnerships.

- New ways to improve customer responsiveness from 95 per cent to 98 per cent.

- New processes in all departments to speed flexibility and reduce costs by at least 15 per cent.

These and other targets then become the metrics that are used to measure creativity and innovation in the company. Note that the objectives do not specify how the goals will be achieved – that is left to teams who will be assigned these objectives. The objectives set ends, not means. They contain some measurable elements and time-lines but are otherwise loose so as to give maximum flexibility.

The vision is important because it underpins all the subsequent planning and direction setting. The flow is shown in Figure 4.2.

Figure 4.2   The flow of vision into objectives and metrics

The setting of strategic goals, and the departmental and personal objectives that cascade down from them, is well understood and executed in most large organizations. There are many books, training courses and methodologies available. However, the setting of innovation objectives and measurements is a neglected part of the strategic planning process. We will explore it later in the book.

Communicating

Just painting the picture is not enough. It quickly fades from view if it is not constantly reinforced. If you want the vision to endure then you must communicate it in many ways. To be an effective leader you have to meet people at all levels in the organization, reinforce the message, solicit their buy-in and gain feedback on their views and concerns. Lateral leaders take time to meet staff, especially new recruits. They illustrate the vision, the goals and the challenges; explain to staff how their role is crucial in fulfilling the vision and meeting the challenges. They inspire people to become crusading entrepreneurs finding innovative routes to success.

Stewart Butterfield is a Canadian serial entrepreneur. He is famous for founding the photo-sharing site Flickr, which he sold to Yahoo. He then developed a gaming application, Glitch, which failed. His latest venture is Slack, a platform for team communication and project management, which has been valued at over US $1 billion. In a recent interview in the *Times of India*, he told of some of the important lessons he has learnt.

When asked what was the one key mantra for a start-up's success he said: 'You need to have clarity of purpose which can be communicated to other people. This makes a huge difference.' He explained that Instagram had a clear and simple message – quick, public photo sharing on mobile. Flickr was less successful because it had a mixed message – it was used for social photo sharing but also by amateur and professional photographers. He believed that the big reason for Glitch's failure was that it was not easy to explain the idea to people.

If you want to succeed with a start-up or indeed with any innovative idea then it helps greatly if you can simply explain exactly what it is. Precisely who will benefit from it and what problem does it solve for them? If this is clear then it makes your marketing clearer and simpler. You can explain your proposition succinctly for investors, suppliers, contractors and staff.

One of the most important qualities that a leader needs is clarity. There must be an open debate about progress and options but once a course is decided then everyone should get on board and pull in the same direction until the next review meeting. Replace confusion with clarity and the team will thank you. The clear purpose of the leader is to create a clear purpose for the team.

In order to transform the organization, you have to use every method of communication to keep people focused on the goals and energized in their search for innovative solutions. At the same time you need to listen carefully to their comments so that you can learn what is working and what is not, and correct the things that are going wrong. It is vital to praise them when they are creative and take risks, because this reassures people that risk taking is part of the corporate culture and that they do not need to fear failure. You need to coach them when they lack the skills or confidence, and inspire them in a dialogue that fully engages their issues and concerns.

New communication methods have opened new avenues for interaction and interchange of ideas. Lateral leaders encourage people to bypass the normal circuitous communication channels and bring important issues quickly to the top. They know that with hierarchical methods of relay messages often get adjusted to suit internal politics.

Jack Welch, the legendary CEO of GE, was an outrageous champion of the corporate vision. This is how he describes it in his book *Jack: What I've learned leading a great company and great people*: 'Whenever I had an idea or message I wanted to drive into the organization, I could never say it enough. I repeated it over and over at every meeting and review. I always felt I had to be "over the top" to get hundreds of people behind an idea' (Welch, 2001).

Welch also understood keenly the importance of communication in fostering an innovative culture:

> Getting every employee's mind into the game is a huge part of what the CEO job is all about. Taking everyone's best ideas and transferring them to others is the secret. There's nothing more important. I tried to be a sponge, absorbing and questioning every good idea. The first step is being open to the best of what everyone, everywhere has to offer. The second is transferring that learning across the organization. Searching for a better way and eagerly sharing new knowledge has today become second nature at GE. (Welch, 2001)

Many managers make the mistake of thinking that communication is a one-way process. They repeat their message but they do not solicit feedback. It is only by consulting either in small groups or individually that you can fully understand whether the message has been received and what concerns and issues it has generated.

Tips for setting and communicating the vision

- Ensure that everyone understands that standing still is not an option.
- Communicate the need for change.
- Paint a goal of where the organization will be. Visualize the benefits.
- If you do not have a clear and meaningful vision statement today then pull together a team to construct one.
- Choose a vision that inspires and directs the organization.
- Ensure that it is broad enough to allow great flexibility.
- Communicate the vision and the messages and strategic objectives that flow from it.
- Derive innovation objectives with measurable targets and deadlines.
- Solicit feedback to draw out concerns and to ensure the vision is properly understood.
- Help people buy into this process by getting them to set their own objectives in line with the vision.
- Use intranet, e-mail, Slack, Whatsapp or whatever is the latest and best tool to achieve unfettered two-way communication.

THE SCHOOL INSPECTION

A schoolteacher knew that the school superintendent would visit the next day. The superintendent would ask questions on spelling or mental arithmetic to the class, and the teacher would choose a pupil to answer. The teacher wanted to give the best impression of the school. What instructions did she give the children in order to create the best impression and maximize the chances that the right answer was given to each question?

05
Making the vision real

Microsoft's only factory asset is the human imagination.
FRED MOODY

Empowering

You cannot deliver the change on your own. The best source for the idea generation and creativity needed for innovation is the team within your organization. To turn people into entrepreneurs who are hungrily looking for new opportunities you have to first empower them. The purpose of empowering people is to enable them to achieve the change through their own efforts. They need clear objectives so that they know what is expected of them. They need to develop the skills for the task. They need to work in cross-departmental teams so that they can create and implement solutions that will work across the organization. They need freedom to succeed. And when you give someone freedom to succeed you also give them freedom to fail. People want to understand and agree what is expected of them. The scope of their freedom and their responsibility must be agreed. They need training, coaching, reinforcement and encouragement. They need support in acquiring creative problem-solving skills and encouragement to be brave enough to come up with radical innovations. Above all, empowerment means trusting people. It is by giving them trust, support and belief that you will empower them to achieve great things.

Empowerment is about more than managers setting objectives and then leaving people alone. It is about encouraging and enabling people to solve problems and seize market opportunities on their own initiatives – either individually or more often in quickly convened groups from different disciplines.

As Roger von Oech points out, studies have shown that the main difference between creative people and others was 'The creative people thought they were creative and the less creative people didn't think they were' (von Oech, 1983: 165). Everyone has the spark of creativity in them. It is the job of the leader to inspire and release that spark.

The goal is to have all individuals think of themselves as entrepreneurs who have the right and the duty to solve problems and seize opportunities – not to offload them to others. In many organizations problems are passed up and down a long chain of command. They are postponed, delegated, transferred, ignored and eventually handled by some remote manager who cannot avoid the issue any longer. In the empowered organization they are handled by the first employee who encounters the problem. This person has the authority to solve problems and take initiatives fast. He or she does not do this in isolation – he or she communicates. The senior team knows what is going on, but because they trust people to do the right things they find out later – after the fact in most cases. This involves risks but it pays back in a much more agile, effective, creative and dynamic mode of operation.

Trust

You cannot empower people if you do not trust them. The lateral leader trusts people to make key decisions in agreed areas. The conventional command and control leader micromanages people. They replace trust with control. An innovation survey among top companies conducted by PricewaterhouseCoopers found that of all the factors that lead to a climate for innovation, the single most important was trust. As they put it, 'The top performers trust empowered individuals to communicate and implement change in order to turn strategic aims into reality.'

Trust takes time. It is something that has to be earned and given. The leader builds a climate of trust over a period. It works best in stable relationships where the leader and the people communicate

well, share common goals and understand the broad limits of responsibility. Trust does not mean that there is no supervision, it means
that people know that they can try different things in order to achieve
common goals. It means that honest failures along the way are
accepted as useful learning experiences.

You build trust by saying what you mean and doing what you say.
People have to know where they stand and they have to know that
you will honour your commitments. If you give them freedom to
make their own decisions then you have to accept the consequences
if things go wrong. Blame and recrimination will destroy trust. It is
essential to keep lines of communication open and active so that you
are in the picture on important developments while allowing day-
to-day decisions to be made by those closest to the action. Set the
strategy, discuss the approach, delegate, trust and communicate.

Overcoming fear

People are anxious about change. Change is uncomfortable. Change
means winners and losers. It is natural that people will prefer to stay
within their comfort zones rather than risk an embarrassing or costly
failure. The lateral leader spends time with people encouraging them
to undertake risks and reassuring them that those risks are necessary
and worth taking. Fear of failure often inhibits people from pushing
themselves to new limits. You have to show that doing nothing has its
risks too; that staying in the corporate comfort zone is a dangerous
option. You have to reassure them that they will not be punished for
taking risks, for worthwhile failures, for bold initiatives that do not
succeed. Of course, taking risks means taking calculated risks, not
wild risks. Every employee who is undertaking a risky initiative needs
freedom, but he or she needs mentoring and guidance too.

Once again communication is the key. Informed people don't fear
change. As Dick Brown, Chairman and CEO of EDS, put it, 'People
are not afraid of change. They fear the unknown.'

Simple reassurance is not enough. You have to let people articulate
their fears and tell you their concerns. It is easy to assume that you
understand people's reactions but it is essential to hear it from them

so that you are addressing the right target. Surveys, intranet bulletin boards and management feedback help, but small group discussions and one-on-one sessions are the best for hearing, understanding and overcoming fear. The fact that you listen shows that you care about your people and their issues. Even if they have heard it all before, leaders listen attentively to the issues that their people raise.

Staying focused

Often it is easier to set an agenda for change than to follow it through to completion. You start out with the best intentions but then you get distracted by urgent matters which have to be dealt with now. In Stephen Covey's book *The Seven Habits of Highly Effective People* (1989), he explains that most people focus on what is urgent (whether it is important or not), but successful people focus also on what is important but not urgent. These are things like building long-term relationships, developing the corporate culture, exploring new opportunities and driving through long-term change. Staying focused on the vision, on making the strategic change happen despite all the pressure of fighting today's fires, is the hallmark of the lateral leader. Most managers understand the need to have two 'to do' lists. One covers the immediate, detailed day-to-day operational items that have to be tackled. The other is the list of strategic goals that need to be addressed over the medium term. It is all too easy to succumb to the temptation to spend long hours on the immediate operational priorities and let the strategic stuff slide. The successful leader will make sure that today's pressing tasks are completed, but will find ways to delegate or prioritize them, such that time is available for the strategic changes and initiatives that will have the big long-term payback.

Planning and preparation

Never satisfied even with success, the lateral leader is constantly looking to develop the business and implement changes. Whether you are changing the corporate culture to be more innovative, restructuring, or implementing innovative products or processes, planning and preparation for the change are essential. They may seem like conventional leadership traits, but lateral leaders ignore them at their peril. Every aspect of the change needs to be thought through and modelled. In addition to the main plan there should be a fallback plan in case the change does not go as well as expected. When Microsoft launches a new version of Windows, the company plans around 100 alternative scenarios to anticipate all the things that could go wrong and how it would handle each one.

'The concept of reversibility is a huge factor in the success of a business,' says Professor Gavin Reid of the University of St Andrews in his study of reasons for the survival or failure of small firms (Reid, 2002: 32). 'Having a Plan B is always a wise decision but a surprising number of entrepreneurs do not even consider it.'

Risks have to be taken but they should be calculated risks. When in the mid-1990s the board of Marconi plc decided to move out of the safe, low-growth and unglamorous business of defence into the exciting growth business of telecommunications, they bet the firm on the outcome. Their timing was most unfortunate. Their arrival in the telecommunications business coincided with a savage downturn in the market that hit the established companies very hard and devastated a newcomer like Marconi, which never recovered.

The lateral leader is like a traveller on a long journey. The traveller knows his destination and has a broad plan of how to get there. He encounters many obstacles, delays and difficulties on the journey, but his resolve to reach the destination never wavers. He is prepared. When one route is blocked, he finds a way around. When his companions lose heart, he reassures them. He motivates them by explaining how good it will be when they get to the destination. He uses their skills and creativity to overcome problems. He leads them home.

Managing the environment

Lateral leaders take care to create the right kind of environment for empowered employees to be creative and entrepreneurial.

They help to set the conditions in which people will feel relaxed, motivated and inspired. There are various ways to do this, depending on the culture and style of your nationality and organization. Usually the atmosphere in the office is informal but dynamic. People are focused and busy working in an environment that encourages easy communication and discourages hierarchies, divisions and 'silos'.

It is commonly assumed that the best way to help people be creative is to put them under pressure. It is thought that if they have a deadline to generate some ideas then that will help the process. But research shows that this is not the case. In a study of 177 employees by staff from Harvard Business School (Amabile, Hadley and Kramer, 2002: 52), it was found that creativity decreased under heavy time pressure. Most people under extreme time pressure felt as though they were on a treadmill and were unlikely to be creative. It was found that people could be creative under time pressure, but only if the leader could inspire them to feel that they were 'on a mission'. They had to share a strong sense of purpose and know that creative endeavours were vital to the outcome. Of course, lack of pressure does not guarantee ideas and innovation. It is easy for people to slip into 'autopilot' mode where they feel no sense of urgency. The authors of the research found that the best results were achieved when people had realistic goals and time to achieve them.

It is wise to design work so that people can concentrate on a single work activity for a large part of the day, rather than chop and change between many urgent tasks. Lateral leaders try to ensure that they have time each day for creative work, and the same applies to the staff. A good example is 3M, which has long had a policy of allowing staff to spend 15 per cent of their time each week on exploring interesting ideas or initiatives outside their assigned work (Amabile, Hadley and Kramer, 2002: 61). Hewlett-Packard has a similar policy. The payback for 3M and HP can be seen in the great flow of new products and innovations that they bring to market.

Using innovation techniques

The lateral leader places great emphasis on finding creative solutions. This is not a haphazard process that is left to a few individuals. It is something that the leader builds into the culture of the organization. This is done by techniques, methods, workshops and a pervading attitude of encouragement for crazy ideas.

The goal is to change the organization; to achieve a metamorphosis from a routine group of people who are doing a job to a highly energized team of entrepreneurs who are constantly searching for new and better ways of making the vision a reality. We want to use creative techniques to drive innovative solutions to reach the goal. But just encouraging innovation is not enough. You need to initiate programmes that show people how they can use creative techniques to come up with new solutions. People need training in order to learn the skills and to develop the confidence to try new methods. We will explore methods and techniques as we go through this book. Innovative leaders lead by example. In the next few chapters we will explore the principles that they use and encourage in others.

Tips for making the vision a reality

- Empower people at all levels by agreeing clear goals and giving them the authority they need to be entrepreneurial in finding ways of achieving their goals.

- Remove fear of the unknown and fear of failure in your words and actions.

- Stay focused on the key strategic goals despite all the day-to-day distractions.

- Create a working environment that encourages creativity.

- Allow people time for exploration and discovery in addition to normal work.

- Plan for success but prepare for setbacks too.
- Invest in employee training. Help them to develop entrepreneurial and creative skills.

BRUSH FIRES

The Los Altos Hills County Fire District commissioners in California had a severe problem with brushwood fires on the slopes of the hills around the town. If they cleared away the brushwood with tractors they could cause sparks which would start fires. What did they do?

06
Challenge your assumptions

The best assumption to have is that any commonly held belief is wrong.
KEN OLSON, CEO, DEC

Only two things are infinite, the universe and human stupidity, and I'm not sure about the former.
ALBERT EINSTEIN

The northern pike is a large freshwater fish that feeds on other fish. One such pike was placed in one half of a glass aquarium, which had a glass partition dividing it. In the other half were many small fish. The pike made repeated efforts to snatch the small fish but hit the glass partition each time and received a painful bump on the nose. The partition was then carefully removed so that all the fish could move around the tank. The pike did not attack or eat the little fish. It had learnt that to attack the little fish was fruitless and painful, so it did not try again. From this story comes the 'pike syndrome' which involves not adapting to changing circumstances and wrongly assuming a complete knowledge of a situation.

We often act like the pike. Every time we approach a problem we bring our accumulated experience and training to bear on it. But this includes our accumulated assumptions and biases – conscious and unconscious. This mental baggage can prevent us from accepting innovative ideas. The natural thing to do is the thing we have always done, but as Charles Ames, CEO of Uniroyal Goodyear, says, 'Blindly following organizational concepts that have worked elsewhere is a sure way to waste talent and get poor results' (Ames, 1990: 2).

Sometimes the way that we frame a problem contains an assumption that prevents us from solving it. In the Middle Ages the definition of astronomy was 'the study of how the heavenly bodies move around the Earth'. The definition implied that the Earth was at the centre of the universe – which was the prevailing view at the time. In about 1510, Nicolaus Copernicus, a Polish astronomer, conceived the idea that the Sun was the centre of the solar system and that all the planets revolved around the Sun, and revolved on their own axes. He did not consent to the publication of his works until after his death because he knew how controversial such views would be.

The idea that the Earth was the centre of the universe was so ingrained into conventional wisdom that it was very hard to displace. Similar ideas exist in most businesses – assumptions that underpin most strategies and decisions, and that are so fundamental that they are never challenged.

Another example of how a definition can contain an assumption that restricts development is the atom. The atom was originally defined as the smallest indivisible unit of matter. The implication was that an atom could never be subdivided. This assumption made it difficult for scientists to conceive of splitting the atom.

The more experienced and expert individuals are, the more likely they are to assume outcomes. Very often an expert will extrapolate from known facts and experiences to predict a result. In 1901, a young Italian radio pioneer, Guglielmo Marconi, came to England to test his theory that radio waves could be transmitted across the Atlantic Ocean. The experts all scoffed at the idea. It was known that radio waves travelled in straight lines, and that the Earth was a giant sphere, so the experts quite reasonably assumed that a radio signal sent flat would travel on a tangent out into everlasting space. Marconi persisted with his madcap experiment, and set up his transmitter in Cornwall and his receiver in Newfoundland. To the world's amazement he succeeded in sending a radio signal across the Atlantic. Unknown to Marconi and to the experts, there was a charged layer around the Earth, the ionosphere, which reflected the radio signals. The experts had based their conclusions on sound facts (radio waves travel in straight lines and the Earth is a sphere) but they had assumed that those facts were sufficient. There were other facts unknown to them that altered the equation.

Henry Ford was a great industrialist who could be an autocratic, conventional leader when needed and an inspiring, lateral leader when needed. He transformed the manufacturing industry with new methods including the production assembly line. The story is told that he took a candidate for a senior position out to lunch. Soup was served, and the candidate added salt to the soup before tasting it. Ford did not hire him. The candidate had assumed the soup needed salt without testing that assumption by tasting the soup. Ford did not want that kind of man, someone who prejudged situations, working for him.

The assumptions we accumulate are like walls that restrict our view of what is possible. We build these walls as we gather our ground rules, assumptions and experiences and hear those of other people. Instead of seeing freely in a 360-degree circle we limit our view to a narrow vista.

After the First World War, the British and French High Commands assumed that any new war with Germany would be similar in nature to the first war – a massive static encounter between two huge armies. So the French built a huge line of defensive fortifications on the border between France and Germany. It was called the Maginot line (after the French Minister of War, M Maginot) and it stretched from neutral Belgium in the north to neutral Switzerland in the south. But when the Germans attacked in May 1940 they did some lateral thinking. The German generals invented a new fast-moving type of warfare, called blitzkrieg, using motorized armoured divisions and paratroops. They swept through neutral Holland and Belgium to go around the Maginot line. France fell in five weeks.

Senior managers are like generals fighting new campaigns using the techniques they learnt in earlier ones. One of the reasons the American forces had difficulties in Vietnam was that the generals fought as though it was Korea (where many had learnt their trade). But each war is different – in technology, in terrain and in technique. And each business problem is different. Making decisions based on assumptions about what worked or did not work before limits you to a restricted choice and can blind you to better solutions.

Banks assumed that certain types of rules must apply for personal loans. There was a minimum amount that could be loaned and security of some kind was needed. In 1983 in Bangladesh, Muhammad Yunus founded the Grameen Bank (meaning 'village bank') to directly challenge conventional assumptions and to make micro loans to poor entrepreneurs. Yunus met strong opposition from anti-capitalist radicals and from conservative imams but the bank proved very popular and made millions of small loans. Grameen fostered an innovative system of 'solidarity groups' of people who band together to apply for loans and who act as co-guarantors of repayment. Their joint informal commitment helps them to build successful businesses and to pay back the debt.

In Bangladesh, Grameen grew to over 2,500 branches lending small amounts to over 8 million borrowers in 80,000 villages. The borrowers were 95 per cent women and the default rate on the loans was less than 3 per cent, which is better than most conventional banks. The success of the Grameen microfinance model has been copied in over 100 countries around the world.

In 2006, Yunus was awarded the Nobel Peace Prize, along with Grameen Bank, for their efforts to create economic and social development. The Nobel Committee said:

> Muhammad Yunus has shown himself to be a leader who has managed to translate visions into practical action for the benefit of millions of people, not only in Bangladesh, but also in many other countries. Loans to poor people without any financial security had appeared to be an impossible idea. From modest beginnings three decades ago, Yunus has, first and foremost through Grameen Bank, developed micro-credit into an ever more important instrument in the struggle against poverty.

In the 1990s Microsoft dominated the PC application software market. In the late 1980s the leading spreadsheet was Lotus 1-2-3, the leading database dBASE III from Ashton-Tate, the leading word processor was WordPerfect and the leading presentation product was Harvard Graphics. By the mid-1990s these had all been replaced by Microsoft products – Excel, Access, Word and PowerPoint. Microsoft had an immensely strong market position with a 90 per cent share of the desktop applications market and it dominated the distribution, reseller and retail channels. Anyone trying to introduce a competing product through the conventional channels would have been turned away. But one small company did find a way to bring a new product to market. Netscape ignored the conventional route to market; it gave away its browser, Netscape Navigator, over the internet and charged for upgrades and professional versions. This fresh approach worked and it became the leader in the browser market. It was as though the distribution channels had been Microsoft's Maginot line and the internet allowed Netscape to outflank the defence and reach the market directly. It took a little while for Microsoft to realize the threat, but once it did, it reacted quickly. Microsoft made its own browser, Internet Explorer, freely available over the internet, then bundled it free with the Windows operating system. Netscape lost its lead role in the browser market and became an internet portal and open software supplier. However, there was another twist when the US Justice Department judged that Microsoft's action in bundling its browser with the Windows operating system was an unfair practice.

The lesson is that when you are competing with a strong market leader you should not necessarily attack head on, but try to change the rules of the game; for example, by approaching the customer from a new direction. When David fought Goliath, he did not use the same weapon as his enemy. If you are facing a giant who has a seven-foot spear then it is no use using a four-foot spear. You need a different approach, and that is what David did with his sling and stone.

Similarly, if you are a market leader, it is dangerous to assume that there are strong barriers to entry which will protect you. An innovative smaller company is probably plotting a surprise attack right now! If your business is in a strong position then you risk slipping into all the assumptions which success can engender. We think we must be doing things right because we are successful. One way to stop yourself from having this mindset is to think of yourselves as underdogs. Phil Knight is the CEO of Nike, who dominate the sports footwear market. He is quoted as saying that although Nike is the Goliath of the industry, it will always behave like the David (Morgan, 1999: 240).

Travis Kalanick had the idea for Uber when he was in Paris in 2009 and could not get a taxi. Most people would just complain or take the bus or metro but Kalanick thought there must be a better way. He challenged the assumption that city transport must involve established infrastructure. He asked, 'Could we harness the capacity of all the drivers in Paris who would be happy to give me a ride for a fee?' Travis Kalanick and Garrett Camp founded Uber, a mobile application that connects passengers with drivers of vehicles for hire and ridesharing services. The company started as a two-car operation in San Francisco and then rocketed upwards. By 2016 it had over 1 million drivers, was delivering over 3 million rides a day in 66 countries, and was valued at US $62 billion. It is claimed to be the fastest-growing start-up in business history. So big was the impact that Uber became a verb meaning to disrupt an entire industry model.

Tips for challenging assumptions

- Recognize that you and everyone else have ingrained assumptions about every situation.
- Ask plenty of basic questions in order to discover and challenge those assumptions.
- Pretend you are a complete outsider and ask questions like 'Why do we do it this way at all?'
- Reduce a situation to its simplest components in order to take it out of your environment.
- Restate a problem in different terms.
- Consider what the experts and professionals advise and then consider doing the opposite.

Use the following exercises to improve your skills in checking assumptions (see Appendix 1):

Exercise F – Break the rules.

Exercise N – Lateral thinking puzzles.

Exercise P – What if?

The greater the expert the more wrong he or she can be, either in assumptions or in negative reactions to new ideas. Here are some classic examples:

Simon Newcomb (1835–1909) was the leading US astronomer of his time and a professor of astronomy and mathematics. He declared that flight by heavier-than-air objects was completely impossible. After the Wright brothers made their first flights he still claimed that aeroplanes were impractical and worthless.

Dr Dionysius Lardner (1793–1859) was Professor of Natural History and Astronomy at London University. He warned that railway trains travelling at speed would asphyxiate their passengers through lack of air. He also stated that no steamship would be able to cross the Atlantic because it would need more coal than it could carry without sinking.

Ernst Werner von Siemens (1816–1892) was the great German engineer who developed the telegraph industry and founded the company bearing his name. He declared, 'Electric light will never take the place of gas.'

Samuel Pepys (1633–1703), the celebrated English diarist, wrote the following comments on seeing plays by Shakespeare. *Romeo and Juliet*: 'The worst play I ever saw in my life.' *A Midsummer Night's Dream*: 'The most insipid, ridiculous play.' *Twelfth Night*: 'A silly play.'

Charles Duell was Commissioner at the US Patents Office, who in 1899 gave his opinion that, 'Everything that can be invented has been invented.'

Ernest Rutherford (1871–1937) was the eminent British physicist who pioneered nuclear physics, discovered the alpha particle and developed the nuclear theory of atomic structure. He refused to believe that nuclear energy could be harnessed and described ideas for nuclear power as 'moonshine'.

Lord Kelvin (1866–1892) was a distinguished British mathematician and physicist who developed the law of conservation of energy. The Kelvin scale of absolute temperature is named after him. He scoffed at the idea of radio and stated, 'Radio has no future.' He also said, 'X-rays will prove to be a hoax.'

H G Wells (1866–1946), the eminent British author and one of the first science fiction writers, said in 1902, 'I refuse to see any sort of submarine doing anything except suffocating its crew and floundering at sea.'

In 1927, H M Warner of Warner Brothers asked, 'Who the hell wants to hear actors talk?'

Irving Fisher was Professor of Economics at Yale University. In 1929 he pronounced, 'Stocks have reached what looks like a permanently high plateau.'

Albert Einstein said in 1932, 'There is not the slightest indication that nuclear energy will ever be obtainable.'

Admiral William Leahy (1875–1959) told President Truman in 1945, 'The atomic bomb will not go off, and I speak as an expert in explosives.'

Rex Lambert, editor of the *Listener*, wrote in 1936, 'Television won't matter in your lifetime or mine.'

John Langdon-Davies, Fellow of the Royal Anthropological Institute, opined in 1936, 'By 1960 work will be limited to three hours a day.'

Sir Richard Woolley was the British Astronomer-Royal who declared in 1956 that, 'Space travel is utter bilge.'

Don Rowe was the director of Decca Records who turned down the Beatles. He said to their promoter, Brian Epstein, 'We don't like your boys' sound. Groups of guitarists are on the way out.'

Frank Sinatra in 1957 stated, 'Rock and Roll is phoney. It's sung, written and played by cretinous goons.'

Ken Olson, CEO of DEC, said in 1977, 'There is no reason anyone would want a computer in their home.'

Bill Gates stated in 1981, '640k ought to be enough for anybody.'

Clifford Stoll, speaking about the internet in 1995, claimed, 'No online database will replace your daily newspaper, no CD-ROM can take the place of a competent teacher and no computer network will change the way government works.'

THE COCONUT MILLIONAIRE

A man buys coconuts at £5 a dozen and sells them at £3 a dozen. Because of this he becomes a millionaire. How?

07
Ask searching questions

It is better to know some of the questions than all of the answers.
JAMES THURBER

I keep six honest serving men
They taught me all I knew
Their names are What and Why and When
And How and Where and Who.
RUDYARD KIPLING

It is your job as a lateral leader to ask fundamental questions about your business and about every situation. It is tempting to appear decisive by jumping straight to the conclusions and making rapid decisions. But the chances are that those rapid decisions are predictable courses based on existing assumptions and prejudices, and that another chance for innovation has escaped.

An old-established and well-known pen company appointed a new VP of Marketing. At the monthly executive meeting, he was faced with this question: How can we increase our pen sales? Sales of the company's top-of-the-market pens had been in slow decline for years. The new man returned to the next month's executive meeting and expressed his opinion that they were asking the wrong question. 'You should be asking, what business are we in?' His colleagues looked at him with disdain. 'We know what business we are in – the pen business.'

'I don't think so,' he replied. 'I have been asking why our customers buy our pens, and I have learnt that they buy our products not as pens but as gifts. When someone retires from the office, when a son or daughter graduates from college or as a Christmas present for Dad – our pens are given as gifts. We are not in the pen business but the gift business. We should change our pricing, our promotions, our distribution and our marketing to recognize this.' They did, and they were much more successful.

The lateral leader needs an abnormally large sense of curiosity. You must question every aspect of the business as though you were a consultant or a new hire on your first day in the company. The longer we have been there the harder this is to do. On our first day at work we ask dozens of questions: Why do we do this? How do we make this happen? What is the purpose of this? What does this mean? The longer we are in the job, the fewer questions we ask, the more assumptions we make and the more complacent we become. You have to keep asking the basic questions and keep listening carefully to the answers. If you put the same question to different people at different times you will get different answers – and those answers contain clues to what has changed. More probing questions and more careful listening are the best ways to give you the deeper understanding you need.

A major French construction company came up with an interesting approach to this problem. They ask every new employee to complete an 'astonishment report' after they have been in the company for a few weeks. The report lists anything that the employee has found astonishing – be it good or bad. The point is that the newcomer sees things that the incumbent takes for granted. Only the immigrant can see what is astonishing – everyone else thinks it is normal.

Intel's main business was making memory chips, but fierce competition from Japan turned memory into a commodity with tiny margins. Intel's founders, Andy Grove and Gordon Moore, sat down and asked themselves some tough questions. 'If we were kicked out and the board brought in a new CEO,' Grove asked, 'what do you think he would do?' 'Get out of the memory chip business,' was Moore's answer. From that insight came the plan to move from memory chips into the higher added-value business of designing and making processor chips (Charan and Useem, 2002: 41). In order to help them think like a new team that had just been appointed, Grove and Moore fired themselves in a virtual sense. They walked out of the building in their old personas and walked back in thinking of themselves as newly appointed to the jobs. It was by asking this kind of question and approaching the problem afresh that Grove and Moore could make the transition that would transform the business. That is lateral leadership in action.

It is important to question the things that everyone else takes for granted, as rules that cannot be broken, as fixed parameters that can never be challenged. When Sir Isaac Newton asked the question, 'Why does an apple fall from a tree?' people must have given him some funny looks. Everyone knew that things fell to the ground, so what was the point of asking why? But Newton persisted. If an apple falls to the Earth why does the Moon not fall to the Earth? Why do the tides ebb and flow? By asking these searching questions Newton was able to conceive his theory of gravitational attraction and his laws of motion.

The kinds of questions a lateral leader asks:

- Are we asking the right question?
- Why do we need to solve this problem?
- Why do we do things this way at all?
- How can we restate the problem?
- What if we reversed the problem?
- Who would benefit and who would lose if we solved this problem?
- What are the rules of our business and what would happen if we broke those rules?
- What are we assuming about this situation?
- What would happen if we challenged those assumptions?
- Can we draw a diagram or picture of the problem?
- Can we model the problem?
- How would someone from another planet solve this problem?
- If we had unlimited money and resources how would we solve this problem?

- How would someone in a completely different line of business solve this problem?
- How can we look at this in a different way?

All the great scientific discoverers had questioning minds. Charles Darwin asked the question, 'How can the different islands of the Galapagos have so many different and unique species of animals?' From his questioning and painstaking research he was able to construct his theory of evolution by natural selection – possibly the most powerful and influential idea ever conceived.

By asking 'What would the world look like if I rode through it on a beam of light?' Albert Einstein was able to create his theory of relativity. He imagined a different view of the universe. Can you use the power of your imagination to conceive an entirely different view of your business? Start by asking the fundamental questions that a Newton or Darwin or Einstein might ask.

Imagination and knowledge

Einstein famously said, 'Imagination is more important than knowledge.' But we put much greater store on knowledge. Most of a child's time at school is devoted to the acquisition, retention and testing of knowledge. Children learn methods and facts and are then tested on how well they can apply those methods and remember those facts. How much time is spent on developing the child's imagination? How much time do we spend teaching thinking as a skill? It is far too little.

Knowledge is important, but it was not knowledge that enabled Michael Cullen to conceive of the supermarket. It was his imagination. Thinking skills, creativity and imagination are the keys to creative problem solving. One of the most important creative skills we need to learn is the art of questioning. We should question everything, every cherished assumption, every rule and method of the business. We should start by asking the fundamental questions a child or a Martian would ask: Why do we do this at all? Why do we do it this way? By challenging the most basic tenets of the organization and the way we do things we can prepare the ground for a crop of creative new ideas.

Creating a questioning organization

Lateral leaders ask very many fundamental questions. They also strive to ensure that everyone is asking questions. Everyone is encouraged to ask how things could be done differently, and how things could be made better. Despite the fact that the company is already achieving great things, it is essential to instil a questioning attitude: How could we be even better? If 'only the paranoid will survive' then we must engender a level of paranoia in the organization. We are doing well, but the threat from the competition and from new entrants is very real. The lateral leader ensures that everyone understands the vision and goals of the enterprise, that people are empowered to achieve, and that they know they have to question every rule and assumption, every established way of doing things if they are going to initiate the creative changes that the organization needs.

Most people ask one or two questions and then rush straight towards a solution. It is a natural tendency – we think we understand the issue and our keen managerial problem solving urges are unleashed. It is natural and fatal. With an incomplete understanding it is very easy to jump to the wrong conclusions: for example, that the problem is how to sell more pens. It is only by holding back and asking question after question that we can explore the situation fully and find more solutions and more creative solutions.

Tips for asking questions

Start with open-ended questions that elicit a wide range of answers rather than closed questions, which can be answered yes or no. So instead of, 'Is our marketing generating enough leads?' (answer – no) it is better to ask, 'How can we generate twice as many leads?'

It is often useful to start with challenging 'How' questions, such as:

- How can we create a new product that delivers twice the customer value?
- How can we cut our inventories in half?
- How can we recruit the best staff?

- How can we reach new prospects?
- How can we cut our cost base by 25 per cent?
- How can we cut waiting times in half?

These questions mean that an incremental or marginal improvement is not enough. We are looking for significant improvements.

When you are probing a situation or problem, a string of linked 'Why' questions can be revealing. For example, consider this question and answer sequence:

Why do people buy our hairdryers?

To dry their hair.

Why do they dry their hair?

Because it is wet.

Why is it wet?

Because they washed it.

Why did they wash it?

To make it look clean.

Why else?

To make it look beautiful.

Why do they want it to look clean and beautiful?

To feel good and to look attractive.

So our hairdryers help customers feel good and look attractive. This prompts more open-ended questions like:

How can we show people that our products will make them feel good and look attractive?

Who is this message targeted at?

Good exercises from Appendix 1 to encourage questioning techniques include: ·

Exercise A – Brainstorming.

Exercise N – Lateral thinking puzzles.

Exercise P – What if?

Exercise R – Remote architects.

People who do not check assumptions and are not good at asking questions often show these behaviours and characteristics:

- They jump to conclusions.
- They are impatient to offer solutions.
- The do not pay attention to other people's ideas.
- They are poor listeners.
- They have a strong desire to get things sorted out quickly.
- They think that action is always progress.
- They have closed minds.
- They never admit that they do not know the answer.
- They do not solicit other people's views.
- They rarely ask for help or admit to mistakes.

If you show some of these characteristics, try the following five-point plan:

1 Slow down a little in your decision making. This does not mean avoiding decisions, but taking a little more care over them.

2 Ask lots of basic questions.

3 Ask for more input and consult more with colleagues before selecting solutions.

4 After you come up with a good idea, try to find two or three better ones.

5 If you do not know the answer, admit it and ask others for help. This is a sign of strength, not weakness.

WRONG NUMBER

The marketing department of a major bank prepared a direct mail campaign to launch a new product. They printed over 2 million brochures but were horrified to find a mistake in the brochure – it had a wrong digit in the telephone number. Callers would get a dead line instead of the call centre. What should they do first – fire the marketing manager or reprint the brochures?

08
Take a different view

You cannot look in a new direction by looking harder in the same direction.
EDWARD DE BONO

Have you ever been in a wood that just looked like a random assortment of trees, then when you take a few steps to the side you see that all the trees are laid out in neat rows? Sometimes we are standing in the wrong place to see an obvious answer. We have to deliberately take a different point of view, come at the problem from a new direction before we have a chance of creating a radical solution.

In 1968, the audience at the Olympic Games in Mexico City was amazed to see a young man take the high jump with his back to the bar. All the other competitors used the time-honoured Western Roll approach of jumping with their face and stomach brushing the bar. The time was ripe for a young American, Dick Fosbury, to ask a fundamental question: 'Is there a better way to perform a high jump?' He experimented and found that there was. He won the gold medal and transformed the sport. He questioned the prevailing assumptions and approached the problem from a new and lateral direction. His was truly a leap of the imagination.

Henry Ford took a different view to assembling motor cars. Traditionally the car would be assembled in one place, with different workers coming along to fit the engine, the gearbox, the dashboard, the brakes and so on. He asked, 'What would happen if instead of the workers moving to the car, the car moved to the workers?' His radical idea was the car assembly line. It enabled the standardized mass production of cars at a much lower overall cost.

Albert Szent-György, who discovered vitamin C, put it this way: 'Genius is seeing what everyone else sees and thinking what no one else has thought.' If you can survey a situation from a different viewpoint then you have a good chance of gaining a new insight. This is what Michael Cullen did. He took a different view in inventing the supermarket, when he imagined turning the shop around so that customers served themselves.

Add together these numbers in your head: 398, 395, 396, 399. If you add them the conventional way then it is a taxing piece of mental arithmetic. But if you notice that they can be rewritten as $400 - 2$, $400 - 5$, $400 - 4$ and $400 - 1$ then it is easy to see the total is $1600 - 12 = 1588$. If we take a slightly different view of the problem or restate it in a different way it becomes much easier to solve.

How can we force ourselves to take a different view of a situation? We are so used to seeing it from one perspective that it is difficult to force ourselves. Instead of looking at the scene from your view, try each of these views:

- the customer's view;
- the product's view (imagine you are the product);
- a supplier's view;
- a child's view;
- a poet's view;
- a comedian's view;
- a dictator's view (take your pick of authoritarian tyrants!);
- an anarchist's view;
- an architect's view;
- Salvador Dali's view;
- Leonardo da Vinci's view;
- Charles Darwin's view.

There are other techniques for forcing different viewpoints, and we will cover some of them in later chapters.

Cyrus McCormick was the inventor of the mechanical reaper. It was a productive labour-saving device that every farmer needed. Unfortunately, the farmers in America in the middle of the 19th century had very little money and could not afford to buy the new machines. So Cyrus took an innovative approach and invented instalment payments so that farmers could pay out of future revenues rather than from their meagre savings.

If you had to study a valley, how many ways could you look at it? You could look up and down the valley, you could scan it from the riverside, or stand and look across it from each hillside. You could walk it, drive along the road or take a boat down the river. You could study a satellite photo. You could peruse a map. Each gives you a different view of the valley, and each adds to your understanding of the valley. Why do we not do the same with a business problem? Why do we immediately try to frame a solution before we have approached the problem from multiple differing perspectives?

The great guru of lateral thinking is Edward de Bono. He describes how he consulted with Ford Motor Corporation about how they could compete more effectively in Europe (de Bono, 1992: Intro). De Bono's idea was very innovative. Ford approached the problem of competing from the point of view of a car manufacturer, and asked the question, 'How can we make our cars more attractive to consumers?' De Bono approached the problem from another direction and asked the question, 'How can we make the whole driving experience better for Ford customers?' The answer he came up with was to ensure that they could always park in congested cities. His advice was that Ford should buy up car parks in all the major city centres and make them available for Ford cars only. The idea was too radical for Ford, which saw itself as an automobile manufacturer with no interest in the car park business.

In the 1950s the freight shipping business was in decline. Cargo ships were expensive to build and run. They spent a long time in harbour waiting for unionized dockers to unload and then load them. Airfreight was rapidly taking market share. For years the industry had tried to reduce costs, but this was not the answer. A different approach was needed, and it came with containerization. If the cargo was loaded into containers, most of the work could be done before the ship arrived in harbour. The vessels achieved much faster turnarounds and therefore their cost-effectiveness was dramatically increased. New efficient container ports sprang up which were not riddled with old-fashioned practices.

The European laundry detergent market is dominated by Unilever, whose main product is Persil, and Procter & Gamble, who market Ariel. For years the fierce competition between these two leading brands of washing powder had been based on advertising and retail channels. In 1998 Unilever took a different approach and innovated by introducing Persil tablets. These concentrated forms of the detergent offered greater user convenience because they were pre-measured and did not involve pouring powder from a large pack. It is reported that Persil gained an extra 10 per cent market share by being first to market with this innovation. Consumers liked the novelty and convenience of tablets, which now represent over 30 per cent of the market (Euromonitor, 2002).

De Bono's advice to Ford, the containerization of freight and the introduction of tablets to replace washing powder all represent different views of a traditional business. And it was by taking a different view that major innovations were achieved. Force yourself to reframe the problem, to break down its components and assemble them a different way, and sometimes a better solution becomes apparent.

Visual links

A good way to reframe a problem is to draw the key term and as many visual links as you think relevant. This helps to structure and restructure your thoughts. It is sometimes called visual brainstorming. Tony Buzan developed this idea into a concept called mind mapping (Buzan, 1993). It works well for individuals and can be used in groups.

In a simple form, it works like this. In the centre of a large piece of paper write the key objective and draw an oval around it. Then write the key attributes of the issue on branches leading out from the oval. Each branch will trigger other branches and sub-branches until a visual map is laid out with all your main thoughts shown and linked. Then you can use a highlighter pen to underline key points and to link related points from different branches. In this way you can see new connections, combinations and ideas.

Say for example the problem you are wrestling with is how to select a new sales office location. You would write the issue in the centre and then write some of the key parameters around it, as shown in Figure 8.1 below.

Now we expand on each parameter with as many secondary points as we think are needed (see Figure 8.2). This is where you often find you should have started with a larger piece of paper!

Figure 8.1   A mind map

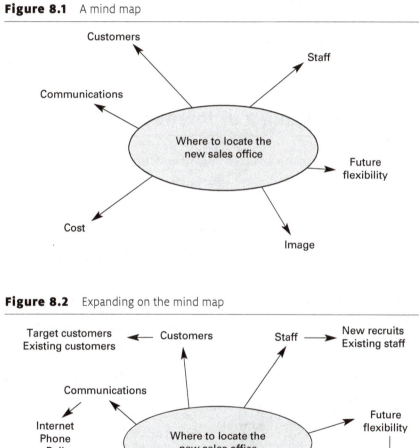

Figure 8.2   Expanding on the mind map

Now we can draw links and add further branches. So we might draw a coloured link between relocation and cost, or between target customers and growth. As you add more links and branches the map becomes messier, but the ideas it triggers become more valuable. The map helps you to visualize relationships between different factors, and to approach the problem from multiple angles.

Also, once you have the parameters and thoughts down on paper, you can then stretch them, exaggerate them, reverse them, challenge them, combine them and integrate them. You can focus on the most promising and brainstorm around them. The whole process helps categorize, structure and define your issues. As such it is an excellent starting point for some of the creative exercises given later in the book.

Tips for adopting a different point of view

- Force yourself to approach the problem from a fresh direction.
- Put yourself in the shoes of a customer, or the product itself or a Martian!
- Reframe the problem – describe it in different words.
- Make a visual representation of the issue with a drawing or with Visual Links.
- Discuss your situation with friends in very different walks of life.
- Start with a random object or word and force an association with the problem.

Use the following exercises in Appendix 1 to help you and your team to take a different view:

Exercise C – Restate the problem.

Exercise D – Similes.

Exercise H – Idea cards.

Exercise I – Found objects.

Exercise V – What's on television tonight?

Exercise Y – Personalities.

Do the opposite

Innovation means taking a different view and what could be more different than the exact opposite? If your current plans and policies are not working then try doing the complete opposite.

The policy of all major software companies such as Microsoft, Oracle and IBM, was to protect their intellectual property. Only a handful of loyal employees were allowed access to the full source code of major software programs and steps were taken to ensure that the valuable programming secrets never left the companies' sites. Linus Torvalds, a Finnish programmer, decided to do the opposite. He created an operating system, Linux, so that anybody could view and amend the source code. This meant that anybody could effectively own and change the software. It was difficult if not impossible to control but that did not worry him because it also unleashed a wave of free creativity and innovation. He created the open source movement by doing the opposite of all the big players.

The movie *The Artist* won the best picture award at the 2012 Oscars. The director had deliberately opposed conventional movie making by filming *The Artist* in black and white and without dialogue.

Jean-Claude Killy was a French downhill skier who wanted to win gold in the Winter Olympics. But he could not do it using the conventional methods so he did the opposite. Everyone was coached to keep their skis together and their weight forward going downhill. He created a new style called *avalement*, which involved keeping the skis apart and sitting back on the skis. He won three gold medals at the 1968 Olympics.

When Anita Roddick founded the Body Shop retail chain she did the opposite of her major rivals. They all presented their perfumes and shampoos in expensive bottles and plush packaging. She used cheap plastic bottles and simple packaging to stress that the contents were what mattered – and that they were pure and simple.

We are all plagued by e-mails from scam artists who tell us we have won the lottery or can help them move millions out of some obscure bank account. The conventional advice is to ignore these e-mails. But what if we did the opposite? What if we all responded by asking for more details? The scammers, who send out millions of e-mails, would be overwhelmed and unable to cope.

Look at your current policies and strategies. What would happen if you did the exact opposite?

TWO CITIES

Which city always contains truth and which city always contains falsehood?

09
Combine the unusual

The simple secret of my genius is that I created something new out of the ideas and inventions of others.
HENRY FORD

The vast majority of new ideas are not original but derived from something else. Most great ideas are really combinations of other ideas. What is the greatest invention ever conceived by human beings? One strong contender for this title is Johannes Gutenberg's printing press. Before Gutenberg, all books had been laboriously copied out by hand or stamped out with fixed woodblocks. Around 1450 in Strasbourg, Germany, Gutenberg combined two existing ideas to invent a method of printing with movable type. He coupled the flexibility of a coin punch with the power of a wine press. His invention allowed the rapid reproduction and distribution of books and pamphlets that powered the spread of knowledge and ideas throughout the Western world.

Gregor Mendel was an Austrian monk who combined mathematics and biology to create the science of genetics. Working in a small monastery garden in the 1850s, he crossed different varieties of peas to see which characteristics were inherited. He conceived the idea that the inherited traits were based on pairs of units that we now know as genes, and that these genes followed simple statistical laws. His great achievements went unnoticed in his lifetime and his genius was recognized only in the early 1900s some 20 years after his death.

3M corporation had a problem with a glue it had invented; it did not stick things together effectively. Then one of its chemists, Arthur Frye, thought of a way of combining the glue with a bookmark, which is something you want to move from page to page, so a glue that did not stick too strongly would be appropriate. His combination was the Post-it note.

When you combine two ideas to make a third, two plus two can equal five. Hydrogen and oxygen are gases but when they are combined they form water. In the ancient world one of the great discoveries was that by combining two soft metals – iron and tin – you could create a strong alloy, bronze. In a similar way, combining two minor inventions – the coin punch and the wine press – gave birth to the mighty printing press.

Try combining your main product or service with a random list of nouns and see what you get. For instance, say you are an architect designing houses and you select the following random list of words from a dictionary: cable, beggar, cartilage, shield, legislature. Forcing combinations might trigger the following sorts of ideas:

Cable: a house with internet cabling built in for every room.
Beggar: houses designed like ancient almshouses, which were for
   the poor.
Cartilage: a flexible hinge like the cartilage in a joint to replace
   conventional hinges.
Shield: an external wall covering that gives extra protection against
   the weather.
Legislature: an imposing front to a house based on the classic
   courthouse.

This approach is guaranteed to get you thinking in new ways and to generate original ideas. Take it further by combining your product with random animals, countries, vehicles, television personalities and so on. The more bizarre the combination, the more original the ideas that are triggered.

Weird combinations are sometimes the strongest

Consider this list of self-contradictory inventions:

- the solar-powered torch;
- the underwater hairdryer;
- the inflatable dartboard;

- the concrete life raft;
- the waterproof teabag.

They are all perfectly possible. For example, the solar-powered torch can be left out in the sun to charge and then taken down a mine. A hairdryer in a submarine is an underwater hairdryer. You could use an inflatable dartboard with Velcro darts. A concrete life raft is certainly possible if it had a large enough air cavity. If a teabag was waterproof at normal temperatures but absorbed water at temperatures near boiling, it would stay fresher in the kitchen before use. The point here is that seemingly ridiculous and contradictory combinations can lead to unusual, workable solutions.

Trevor Baylis is the English inventor who came up with the idea of a clockwork radio. At first this combination seems bizarre. Radios need electricity and clockwork is a mechanical method. Surely batteries or mains electricity are better ways to power a radio. But in many developing countries, batteries are expensive and mains electricity is unreliable. By building a clockwork drive for a tiny generator in his radio, Baylis was able to give people a reliable radio that they could wind up by hand. It transformed the availability of information throughout many of the poorest regions of the earth.

The combination of ideas may be as mundane as putting a clock together with an alarm and getting an alarm clock, as the inventor Levi Hutchins did; or it could be as sophisticated as the work of Gregor Mendel. The fact is that nearly every new idea is a synthesis of other ideas so it makes sense to force combinational possibilities.

When we consider weird combinations, the concept does not just apply to products and services – it applies to organizations too. The Irish rock band U2 performed with the operatic tenor Pavarotti. They married two completely different musical genres. Each brought a new audience to the other's music and their joint concerts and CDs were a big success. When Mercedes Benz wanted to develop an entirely new concept of town car they chose to collaborate not with another engineering company but with Swatch, the fashion watch manufacturer. Together they came up with the Smart car – the most innovative small car since the Mini.

The idea of collaboration works for businesses large and small. A supplier of camellias cooperated with a conservatory manufacturer.

He noticed that the conservatories in the showroom were empty. By putting his camellias on display in the conservatories he found a great way to display his products and to enhance the look and feel of these glass constructions.

Tips for forcing combinations

- Take your main product or service and force-fit a connection with each item on a list of random products, services or objects.
- Look for combinations between your organization and every other organization you come across. How could we collaborate with company XYZ to deliver a radical new offering to clients?
- What is the silliest thing you can put with your product or business? Start from there.
- Study how your customers use your products or services. What do they use them with? Is there a combination you could create which would make their lives easier?

Use the following exercises in Appendix 1 to practise generating combinations:

Exercise B – Random word.

Exercise H – Idea cards.

Exercise I – Found objects.

Exercise K – Roll the dice.

THE STOCKBROKER

A young stockbroker was starting his own practice. He had no clients. How did he convince a small number of wealthy people that he could accurately predict stock price movements?

10
Adopt, adapt, improve

A ship is safe in the harbour but that is not what ships are for.
ALBERT J NIMETH

Closely allied to the concept of combining different ideas is the concept of adapting ideas that have worked in one environment and using them in another. It is one of the most successful of innovation techniques. Let's look at some examples.

In 1916, a young American scientist and inventor called Clarence Birdseye went to Canada as a fur trader. He noticed that people in Labrador kept their food frozen in the snow for extended periods in the winter. When he returned to the United States he developed this idea, launched a line of quick-frozen foods and persuaded retailers to stock them in freezers. He created the frozen food industry. Birdseye subsequently sold his business to General Foods Corporation and made his fortune. He saw a good idea, adapted it to his business environment and implemented it.

Alexander Graham Bell studied the workings of the human ear. He adapted the idea of the eardrum vibrating with sounds into the workings of a metal diaphragm, which led to his invention of the telephone.

The motto of the Round Table is 'adopt, adapt, improve', and it is an excellent guideline for implementing new ideas in your business. Taking ideas from other environments and adapting them for use in your situation is one of the best ways of implementing novel solutions. Amar Bhide of the Harvard Business School studied the origin and evolution of new businesses. He found that over 70 per cent of successful start-ups were based on ideas that the founders had adopted from their previous employments. They took a promising idea in a field they understood and made it better (Bhide, 1999).

An example is Bob Metcalfe who worked at Xerox PARC, the famous research centre which has been the source of many great inventions. In the 1970s he worked on a networking idea called Ethernet which could link computers together. He was sure it was a great commercial opportunity but the directors of Xerox PARC disagreed so he left and founded his own company, 3Com, which became a huge success in the Local Area Networking (LAN) market.

A similar experience befell Dan Bricklin, who developed the idea of the spreadsheet while working at DEC. When he could not convince his superiors to back the idea he quit DEC and founded his own company, Visicorp. He developed the world's first spreadsheet, Visicalc. It became a bestseller and he eventually sold the company to Lotus.

The person who invented the roll-on deodorant was looking for a new way to apply a liquid. He copied an idea from another field, writing, where the same problem is solved. He adapted the concept of the ballpoint pen to create the roll-on deodorant.

A great way for you to innovate is to copy someone else's idea. Adapt it and implement it in your business. Find out what people in your line of business do in different areas, countries and continents. Pinch their best ideas. Borrow ideas from other industries – if it worked for them it might work for you. An idea which is routine in another field might be revolutionary in yours. Just like the roll-on deodorant.

Samuel Morse was the inventor of Morse code. He encountered a problem sending signals over long distances on the telegraph: the signal became attenuated and weak. Then one day when he was travelling by stagecoach he noticed how the coach changed horses at relay stations. He adapted this idea to put in relay stations for telegraphs that boosted the signal.

In 1941, George de Mestral went for a walk with his dog in the Jura mountains in Switzerland. On their return, he noticed that many plant burrs were attached to his trousers and to the dog's coat. They were hard to remove. He examined them under a microscope and saw that they contained tiny hooks which caught in the loops of his clothes and in the dog's hair. He developed an artificial material to mimic nature and in doing so he invented Velcro.

If you have a problem, try to force-fit a link with a random event or animal or institution. Then adapt some ideas from that environment. Say your problem is how to motivate a lethargic team and you choose at random the Olympic Games, a tiger and a ballet school. What sorts of ideas would that trigger? You might offer medals as recognition for top performers. You could keep records of who has achieved the fastest qualified lead or the fastest assembly time, and post them on the wall or the extranet in the form of Olympic records. The tiger might suggest face painting as a trick for raising morale, or it might suggest hunting; you could have a treasure hunt in the office or organize a 'hunt for sales' competition. And so on. The ballet school students practise all their exercises each day before they perform a dance. This might suggest a high-energy group practice session each morning before work proper begins. Ballet dancers practise in front of mirrors; what if we installed systems that gave us feedback to build the team's motivation?

Alternatively, try to adapt a combination between your organization's main strength and that of other organizations or people. Say you provide high-level training courses and you choose at random a hospital. You might come up with the idea of a consulting accident and emergency clinic where people turn up with their problems and you help diagnose them on the spot. Or you may ponder that many people forget what they learn on training courses. In a hospital, patients have ongoing physiotherapy sessions to aid recovery. This idea could be adapted so that you send out 'physio trainers' to top up the learning of participants after they have completed their courses. Alternatively, if you think of the Boy Scouts, then you might imagine a summer camp for some of your top clients or a 'bob a job' campaign where you offer short introductory courses for new clients.

It is very likely that the current problem you face at work today has been faced and solved by other people. Maybe they were in your line of business, or maybe they confronted a similar problem but in an entirely different walk of life. Why do all the brain work yourself when you can adapt someone else's idea and make it work for you?

Tips for finding ideas you can adopt and adapt

- Deliberately gather inputs from unrelated settings.
- Take time out to discuss your problem with people from entirely different backgrounds. If you are a businessperson then ask a teacher or a priest or a musician.
- Read a different magazine, visit a different environment, see a foreign movie, drive a new route home, find some new inspiration in a different source.
- Place yourself in a different environment and it will help you see concepts and ideas you can adapt. If you visit an Inuit in an igloo, like Clarence Birdseye, you may come back with an idea as good as the one that built the frozen food industry.
- Identify analogous situations in other fields and ask how they would be handled.

Exercises from Appendix 1 that can help prompt you to find ideas you can adapt are:

Exercise D – Similes.

Exercise H – Idea cards.

Exercise V – What's on television tonight?

Exercise W – Scamper.

Exercise X – Transformers.

Exercise Z – The ideas board.

THE UNUSUAL

What can you dry your hair with, cut the grass with and lift a car with?

11
Break the rules

Man can live without air for a few minutes, without water for a few days, without food for a few weeks – and without a new thought for years on end.
KENT RUTH

Apple introduced its hand-held assistant, the Newton, in the early 1990s. It was a radical innovation and it used an emergent technology – handwriting recognition. You wrote onto the screen and the software was meant to understand your writing. Unfortunately it did not work well. Getting software to understand different people's handwriting proved to be extremely difficult. Several other companies tried and failed. Then Palm changed the rules. It innovated with a special text input technique called Graffiti. Instead of the PDA (personal digital assistant) learning to recognize your writing you had to learn the Graffiti style of writing, then it all became easy. People were much better at adapting and learning than computers were.

If you can find a way to change the rules of the game so that it suits you rather than your competitors, that change can give you a unique advantage.

Heinz had a problem with its tomato sauce. It was so thick that it poured very slowly out of the bottle, and customers had to jerk the bottle hard to get the sauce out. Competitors' sauces poured much more easily. Most companies in Heinz's position would have tried to make their sauce less viscous. But Heinz found a different approach. The company turned the problem on its head and made an advantage out of a disadvantage. It changed the advertising to emphasize the slowness of the sauce, and implied that sauces that ran quickly must be of lower quality. It made it look cool to bang the bottom of the bottle to extract the sauce. Subsequently it offered the sauce in squeezable plastic bottles, so you had the choice of squeezing a plastic bottle or tapping the glass one.

How would you go about the challenge of inventing a new sport? You could start with a blank sheet of paper and write down all sorts of crazy ideas. A different and probably more productive route would be to start with an existing game and to see what happens if you break the rules of that game one by one. One of the rules of the game of soccer is that you cannot use your hands. It was the deliberate breaking of this rule that led to the creation of the game of rugby. One of the rules of the game of rugby is that the ball cannot be passed forward. It was the deliberate breaking of this rule that led to the creation of the game of American football. Try it with the game of tennis. What if there were three players? What if the ball could bounce back into play rather than be hit out? What if there was no net? What if there were no rackets? What if the ball could not bounce (like a shuttlecock)? You will quickly see that each rule broken leads to a new type of game, some of which are similar to squash, rackets, lacrosse, badminton and so on.

Just as with sports, often in business it is easier to conceive a new enterprise by breaking the rules of an existing business model than by designing something from scratch. Jeff Bezos of Amazon broke the rules of the book business by using the internet rather than conventional distribution channels. Richard Branson's Virgin Group has upset the established ways of business in various industries. Anita Roddick, founder of the retail chain the Body Shop, succeeded by adopting a policy of deliberately doing the opposite of what the industry experts did. Rules are there to be broken. In sports the referee may penalize you, but in business the marketplace will be the referee and it will reward a rule breaker who creates value through innovation.

In the early 1980s, if you wanted to take out motor insurance in the United Kingdom then you went to a high-street insurance broker who took down all your details on various forms and sent them off to insurance companies to get quotes. Insurance brokers insisted that it took all their skill and experience to eventually get you a good policy. Then Peter Wood came along and took a different view. He bypassed the insurance brokers altogether. His company, Direct Line, used computer databases with up-to-date information, and banks of telephone operators to quote competitive prices immediately over the phone. It rewrote the rules of the industry, and Direct Line grew into the largest UK motor insurance company.

What Peter Wood did was to take telephone and database technologies – neither of which was particularly new at the time – and apply them in an innovative way in order to find a new and better way of reaching and serving the customer. Applying new (or nearly new) technologies to traditional business is a classic way of innovating in a marketplace and of going around competitors' Maginot lines. Amazon did a similar thing when it used the internet to bypass the traditional book-retailing channel in order to sell first books, then CDs and other merchandise direct to users everywhere.

Michael Dell was 18 when he founded his company in 1984. His goal was to take on the mighty IBM and Compaq, who dominated the PC business. They had well-established channels through resellers who held stock and sold it to their customers. Because computers were still seen as complicated, the unwritten rules were that PCs came in standard models supplied through resellers who provided the help and support that customers needed. Dell deliberately broke these rules. He bypassed the channel and sold direct to end users. He allowed users to specify their exact configuration, including for example disk size and memory. The quality of the products was good, so he did not need service engineers on site. Furthermore, by building to order, Dell Computer Corporation was able to reduce its inventories so that while competitors carried 75 to 100 days' worth of sales in stock, Dell carried just four days' worth. In the fast-changing PC business this meant costs were lower and customers benefited from the latest technology.

Another example of breaking the rules came in the US newspaper industry with the story of *USA Today*. Before its launch in 1982, the leading newspaper analyst, John Morton, dismissed its prospects of success: 'The list of large circulation newspapers established since the Second World War is not just short – it is non-existent.' The major newspapers were based strongly in different regions, but *USA Today* went national from day one. The upstart publication broke dramatically with convention by bursting with colour and graphs, and by delivering short articles on popular culture, sports and entertainment. It found a new audience – business travellers who wanted to catch up on the main national and local news over their breakfasts. It found a new way of reaching them, by targeting hotels and airports. When *USA Today* took major share and advertising revenue away from existing giants like the *Wall Street Journal* and the *New York Times* they were forced to add colour, become less stuffy and copy the young pretender (Stein, 2002: 68).

Don Estridge of IBM broke the rules in 1980 when he and his small team designed the IBM Personal Computer. Until then all computers, from IBM and elsewhere, had closed proprietary architectures. The designs were secret and copyrighted. Estridge made the IBM PC an open system so that the specification was accessible to everyone. The machine was made from bought-in, standard available parts, unlike all other IBM computers whose components were made by IBM. When the IBM PC was launched in 1981 it had to compete with the market leader Apple and with rivals from DEC, Wang, Commodore and others. It did not offer a better performance, but because it broke the rules by offering a public specification it became a runaway success. People could easily design and add their own extensions, cards and accessories. It became the standard platform for the whole industry. Steve Jobs was so impressed that he offered Estridge a salary of US $1 million and a signing bonus of US $2 million to become President of Apple, but Estridge turned it down. He died tragically in a plane crash in 1985, but he will always be remembered as the father of the PC.

Ironically the secret of the success of the IBM PC – its openness – became the reason that IBM lost the leadership in the business. Compaq, Dell and others built better clones of the IBM PC and took market share away. Microsoft, which had been chosen by IBM to provide a minor component – the operating system – founded a huge empire based on it.

Just like Apple, Microsoft kept its operating systems closed and proprietary. As mentioned earlier, it was ultimately threatened by the rise of Linux, an 'open source' operating system conceived by a 21-year-old Finnish student, Linus Torvalds, who made the Linux programs freely available to anyone. This meant that the system could be developed and shaped by hundreds of programmers around the world.

The Linux model became a paradigm for a person to break the rules in a totally different industry. In 1989 Rob McEwen became the majority shareholder in an old, under-performing gold mine in Ontario, Canada, called the Red Lake mine. He was sure that high-grade gold ores existed somewhere within his land but he could not discover them. Then at a computer technology forum he heard about Linux and how the operating system's programming codes were available to anyone so that they could propose improvements. He thought he could adapt this idea to the mining industry, so he published all the masses of geological and statistical data about the mine on his website and made it available to anyone. In March 2000, he issued a challenge, the Goldcorp challenge, offering prizes total-ling US $500,000 to people who predicted the best places to drill for gold. The rest of the mining industry was amazed and sceptical. He had broken one of the oldest rules in mining – your exploration and reserves data was sacred and not released to anyone for fear of a hostile takeover. But McEwen was an outsider and brought a radi-cally fresh approach.

His challenge received enormous publicity. Over 1,400 scientists and geologists worldwide downloaded the data and performed virtual explorations. The winners were two groups from Australia, Fractal Graphics and Taylor Wall Associates, who had never seen the mine but had developed powerful 3D graphic models of the mines. Their predictions proved very accurate, as did those of the next four contestants. In 2001, following the challenge, the mine produced 10 times the gold it had previously and at a much lower cost per ounce. By taking a different view, adapting an idea from another field and breaking the rules of the industry, McEwen had achieved a remark-able breakthrough (Tischler, 2002).

Look at the rules in your business

Many of the rules that apply in businesses were set in earlier times and have endured by force of habit. A good example is the QWERTY keyboard, which is in use on all desktop computers. The original QWERTY layout of keys on the typewriter keyboard was designed in the 1870s to slow down the speed of typing, because fast operators were causing typewriter keys to jam together. By putting the most commonly used letters e, a, i, o away from the index fingers of the hands, the designers reduced typing speed and jams were avoided. Those mechanical jams are long gone, but we are stuck with a rule for a keyboard layout that is outdated and inappropriate. How many of the rules in your organization are QWERTY standards – set up for circumstances that no longer apply today?

The British and French high commands thought they understood the rules of war. Hitler broke those rules and went through neutral Holland and Belgium to circumvent the Maginot line. If your business is operating to outdated rules – whether explicit or implied – then a smart competitor can break those rules and find a better way of reaching your customers.

This is what Richard Branson did when he launched Virgin Atlantic to take on the might of British Airways and the American transatlantic carriers such as American and PanAm. The rules then were that first-class passengers enjoyed the best service, business passengers received adequate service and economy passengers got very few frills. Branson eliminated first class and instead gave first-class service to business passengers. He introduced innovations including free drinks for economy passengers, videos in headrests, and limousine service to the airport.

Anita Roddick saw that most pharmacies were stuffy places that sold toiletries, perfumes and medicinal creams in expensive packaging and pretty swirling bottles. She did the opposite by packaging the goods in Body Shop stores in cheap plastic bottles with plain labels.

Travis Kalanick broke the rules of urban transport with Uber. Airbnb broke the rules of hotel booking by offering rooms in people's homes. Snapchat broke the rules of messaging with a message which deletes itself.

Jeff Bezos, the founder of Amazon, is a lateral thinker and rule breaker. Amazon pioneered many innovative practices such as recommending what customers would like based on an algorithm which compared previous buying patterns with those of other consumers.

Although its sales of new books were growing very healthily, in 2002 Amazon introduced a service whereby people could sell second-hand books through the company's website. This was surprising as it appeared that each second-hand book sale meant the loss of a larger-margin new book sale. The move was controversial and Jeff Bezos sent out an open letter explaining Amazon's actions. In it he argued that selling second-hand books was good for customers and therefore good for the industry.

Jeff Bezos realized that there was a potential customer need for an inexpensive reader for electronic books. But Amazon had no experience or competence in electronic product design or manufacture. Amazon's strengths lay in excellent web services, software and logistics. For the company to launch its own hardware product would be a major step into unknown territory. Yet that is what they did in 2007 with the launch of the Kindle. It became a tremendous success.

The company continued to experiment and innovate in a remarkable number of fields. It produced its own TV and film features, and in 2013 it announced plans for drone deliveries. Not all the innovations succeed, however. In 2014 Amazon entered the smartphone market with the release of the Fire Phone, but it was considered to be too gimmicky and it flopped.

In 2004 Elon Musk founded Tesla Motors in order to produce mass-market electric cars and in 2008 he became CEO and product architect. He is a rule breaker who shaped the company's many innovations. He stipulated a carbon-fibre-reinforced polymer body. He took the unprecedented step of opening all the company's electric car patents to outside use, saying, 'We will not initiate patent lawsuits against anyone who, in good faith, wants to use our technology.' Unlike other automobile manufacturers, Tesla Motors sells direct to the public rather than using dealerships. Tesla Motors is palpably different from conventional car companies and this increases its appeal to people who want an alternative and cleaner car.

Bezos, Branson, Musk, Wood, Dell, Estridge, Roddick and McEwen all embodied the characteristics of lateral leaders and were mavericks in their industries. They caused havoc by deliberately breaking the rules and challenging the conventional wisdom.

Tips for breaking the rules

- Recognize that your business has all sorts of unwritten rules that guide and limit you.

- Sit down and write out all the rules which apply in your business.

- Get someone else to add the ones you have missed.

- Keep going until you have a long list and then analyse which, if any, are essential and which are boundaries that can be broken. Chances are you can break most of the rules in some creative way or other.

- List the worst and most outrageous things you could do in your business. Start from there and move towards useful ideas.

- Ask yourself how Richard Branson or Michael Dell would launch a new company in your business. How would they do things differently?

These are good exercises to use from Appendix 1:

Exercise F – Break the rules.

Exercise O – The ideal competitor.

Exercise P – What if?

PRICE TAG

Many shops have prices set at just under a round figure, such as £9.99 instead of £10 or £99.95 instead of £100. It is often assumed that this is done to make the prices appear lower to the consumer. But this is not the reason the practice started. What was the original reason for this pricing method?

12
Analyse first

I really wish I was less of a thinking man, and more a fool who's not afraid of rejection.
BILLY JOEL

Our natural approach when we encounter a problem at work is to come up with an idea and then take decisive action. This is an expected response for an active manager. It is better than doing nothing and it is often a good thing to do. If the building is on fire then you evacuate and call the fire brigade.

However, there are many times when this is not the most suitable approach. Our knee-jerk ideas may well not be the best. More importantly, because we have a poor understanding of the problem, we find ourselves shooting at the wrong target.

Albert Einstein once said that if he had one hour to save the world he would spend 59 minutes analysing the problem and one minute coming up with solutions. But we often do the opposite. If the problem is that sales are down, we talk about it for a minute and then cut the price. Our problem-solving model is simple and unsophisticated:

- think of first idea;
- implement.

A better method is to follow this plan:

- analyse the problem;
- prioritize the key issues;
- focus on one key issue at a time;
- generate many ideas for that;

- evaluate and select the best ideas;
- implement one or more ideas for that topic.

By analysing the problem in one or more groups we can develop a better understanding of the whole problem and all its underlying causes. We can then choose which of the problem causes we want to tackle first, second and third. The analysis helps us to define and comprehend the problem before we start on the creative business of coming up with proposals. The lateral leader knows when to use analytical skills and when to use creative skills.

There are various techniques that work well for problem analysis. Many of them involve a form of mind map as described in Chapter 8. The three methods that follow all fall into this broad category. They help describe the situation and its probable causes in a graphical form. Another powerful problem analysis tool is Six Serving Men, which can be found in Appendix 1. This method forces you to approach the problem from 12 specific and different points of view.

Fishbone analysis

This is a method developed in Japan. A diagram is drawn in the shape of a fish skeleton as shown in Figure 12.1.

In the head of the fish is written the problem. On the main bones are written the main causes of the problem. More main bones can be

Figure 12.1   A fishbone diagram

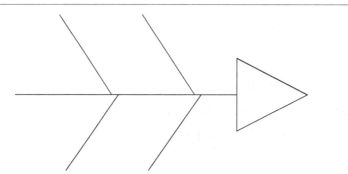

added. Then on ancillary horizontal bones the additional factors for each main cause are written.

Say the problem is poor sales of a new product. This is written in the head. The main reasons are agreed to be that it was launched in the wrong market, there was no commitment from the sales force, it was overpriced and the wrong design. After further discussion of the supporting causes for each of these problems the final diagram might look as shown in Figure 12.2.

It is good to get two or three small groups to do their own Fishbone analysis and then to compare results.

As with all problem analysis techniques, the purpose is not to solve the problem but to understand the underlying causes before attempting to find solutions. It helps people see the overall nature of the problem and the interrelated causes. It can enable you to prioritize which areas to focus on first and then give you a prototype project plan for solving the problem.

The Fishbone method is quick and structured so it is good for groups who have little experience of problem analysis methods.

Figure 12.2   Expanding on the fishbone analysis

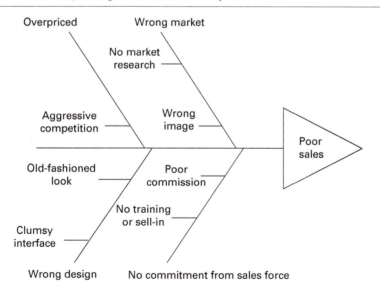

Why, why?

This method is similar to the Fishbone method but with a freer format. The problem is stated and then the question 'Why?' is asked. This should elicit some initial main answers. Then for each of these answers the question 'Why?' is asked again. This process is repeated until a full picture of all the causes is shown.

Say the problem was poor results from brainstorming meetings then the initial Why? diagram might look like Figure 12.3.

The process can be extended for instance by asking why there was no confidence in the process or why there is a risk-averse culture.

The Why, Why? method is similar to the Fishbone method and is a useful alternative. It probably suits more difficult problems and more confident groups than Fishbone.

Figure 12.3   An example of an initial Why? diagram

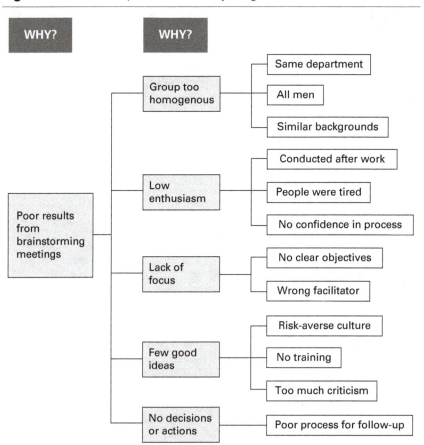

This method encourages us to think like a child. Children often ask 'Why?' and continue to ask until it becomes irritating. It is a highly effective technique for getting to the bottom of an issue but it is one that we abandon when we no longer wish to appear childish. Use this technique to rediscover the power of the child's questioning technique.

Lotus blossom

A more sophisticated version of the problem analysis mapping technique is the Lotus Blossom method, which also originates from Japan.

This method is more thorough than Fishbone or Why, Why? but it takes longer and it requires considerably more paper! It is meant

Figure 12.4   The Lotus Blossom method

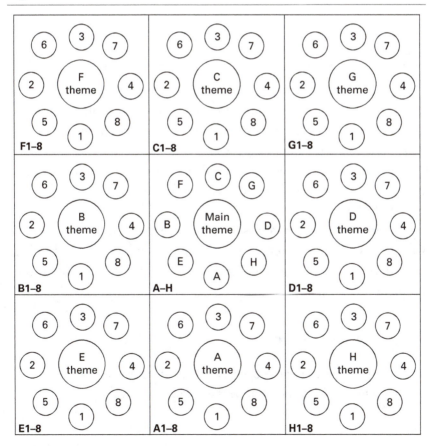

to resemble the peeling of the petals of a lotus blossom flower where each petal reveals more petals underneath.

The problem or issue is written in a circle in the middle of a large piece of paper and the eight main causes of the problem are discussed and agreed. They are drawn as satellites around the main issue.

Each of these eight causes becomes a theme in its own right and the team has to find eight attributes, issues or causes for each. This results in nine sheets of paper, each containing the eight main themes which in turn generate a further eight sub-themes. So we end up with some 64 issues – many of which are interrelated. It is best to start with a big wall for Lotus Blossom!

It may appear heavy handed to force people to find eight causes or attributes for each theme. However, many groups find that the extra effort is worthwhile and that the discipline ensures that the issues are fully explored. Items that would otherwise be overlooked are uncovered.

Cogitate

Once you have defined a problem, it is a good idea to let the subconscious go to work for a while before attempting any solutions. Many great thinkers and inventors have used the following method. They analysed the problem. They parked it for a while and did something else. The result is that they allowed their subconscious mind to digest the issues. Later when they returned to the topic they found they had a well of new ideas.

By separating the analysis and the creation stages of problem solving you form a better view of the situation, you are more likely to find and focus on the real issues, and your brain has time to turn up better solutions.

LOST IN THE DESERT

Two men were lost in a large desert. One started walking due east and the other started walking due west. Two hours later they met.
How?

13
Increase the yield

The best way to get a good idea is to get a lot of ideas.
LINUS PAULING

One of the great problems with our education system is that it teaches that for almost every question there is one correct answer. Examinations with multiple-choice questions force the student to try to select the one right answer and avoid the three wrong answers. So when our students leave school they are steeped in a system that says, find the 'right answer' and you have solved the problem. Unfortunately, the real world is not like that. For almost every problem there are multiple solutions. We have to unlearn the school approach and instead adopt an attitude of always looking for more and better answers.

To be really creative you need to generate a large number of ideas before you refine the process down to a few to test out. To make your organization more innovative you have to increase the yield, then harvest the field. Why do you need more ideas? Because when you start generating ideas you generate the obvious, easy answers. As you come up with more and more ideas so you generate more wacky, crazy, creative ideas – the kinds that can lead to really radical solutions.

The Toyota Corporation in-house suggestion scheme generates over 2 million ideas a year. Over 95 per cent of the workforce contribute suggestions; that works out at over 30 suggestions per worker per year. The most remarkable statistic from Toyota is that over 90 per cent of the suggestions are implemented. Quantity works (Cox, 2001: 100).

Thomas Edison was prolific in his experiments. He said, 'Genius is 1 per cent inspiration and 99 per cent perspiration.' His development of the electric light took over 9,000 experiments and that of the storage cell around 50,000. He still holds the record for the most patents – over 1,090 in his name. After his death, 3,500 notebooks full of his ideas and jottings were found. It was the prodigiousness of his output that led to so many breakthroughs. Picasso painted over 20,000 works. Bach composed at least one work a week. The great geniuses produced quantity as well as quality. Sometimes it is only by producing the many that we can produce the great.

A more recent example of an artist producing many works and varied forms is Madonna. Not only has she written and produced many songs, she has reinvented herself many times. She has not been satisfied with success in one style but has constantly experimented with new forms. She has portrayed herself as a material girl, a virgin, a feminist on the Blonde Ambition tour, an exaggerated sex object, a gay icon, a classical actress in *Evita*, a political activist and so on. Each venture represented a risk that she would alienate her fan base, but the risks have paid off as she has stayed at the forefront while more conventional artists have slipped from the public's consciousness.

When you siphon water from one point to a lower point, the water flows up first before it flows down. Sometimes an idea has to go to a silly level before it can reach a workable level. A company that packed china vases for transit used newspapers as the packing material. The problem they had was that the packers, as they picked the newspapers to screw into balls, would often stop to read interesting articles that they spotted. Various solutions were tried but it seemed that with the boring nature of the packing work it was impossible to stop workers being distracted by the articles. A brainstorming session was held, and one manager suggested the idea of poking the eyes out of the employees to stop them reading. This rather nasty and impossible idea triggered a good idea from another person in the session. Why not employ blind people? The company did this and found that blind people were keen to do the work and made excellent packers. The company had found a better solution and was recognized for its civic contribution.

When you start brainstorming or using other creative techniques, the best idea might not come in the first 20 or the first 100 ideas. The quality of ideas does not degrade with quantity – often the later ideas are the more radical ones from which a truly lateral solution can be developed.

Tips for increasing the yield

- Read the section on brainstorming.
- Set a high target for the number of ideas and then exceed the target.
- Keep the energy level high in your meetings.
- Encourage new ideas.
- Do not criticize new ideas, no matter how silly. Just write them down to start with.
- Analyse and cross-reference ideas using coloured pens.
- Looks for ways to improve, adapt and combine ideas.
- Stop gathering ideas when the energy level drops.
- Use the six thinking hats exercise to analyse the most promising ideas further.

Iterate to innovate

The game Angry Birds was a huge hit for the Finnish game developers, Rovio Entertainment. It sold over 20 million copies on various mobile platforms. The spin-off products include books and a Sony film. Angry Birds was released in 2009, and was the 52nd game that Rovio had launched since the company was founded in 2003. There were 51 earlier attempts before the big hit arrived.

WD-40 is a widely used lubricant and penetrating oil. It was developed in 1953 by a chemist, Norm Larsen, in San Diego. The term WD-40 is derived from 'Water Displacement, 40th formula'. It was the 40th formula the chemists had tried before finding success. The product is produced by the Rocket Chemical Company and is distributed in over 160 countries. The formula for WD-40 is a closely guarded trade secret.

Many great products were the result of a long series of iterations. The first release is rarely an immediate winner. Innovation is a process of continuous improvement and sometimes of trial and error with multiple failures eventually leading to success.

We see a similar process in the arts and in business. The novel *Harry Potter and the Philosopher's Stone* by J K Rowling was rejected by 12 publishers before it was accepted. *Gone with the Wind* by Margaret Mitchell was rejected 38 times. The founders of Skype made 40 investor pitches before they were accepted. Cisco made 76 and Google around 350. Rejection is part of the process – but only if it is used to trigger learning and improvement. Authors whose pet project is rejected have to rework and improve their pitch. So did Larry Page and Sergey Brin. They treated each rejection as a step along the road and a chance to refine their presentation for the next investor.

Everybody wants their first big idea to be a success. But it is much more likely to be a flop, albeit an educational flop. The Jacuzzi brothers launched a bath with inbuilt water jets, designed to ease the pain of sufferers from arthritis. The target market liked the product but could not afford it so it was a commercial failure. Sometime later the brothers relaunched the product but this time aimed at rich people with the benefit not of relieving pain but of improving social life. This time it was a big success.

How can you avoid the pain of launching a product only to see it flop? One approach is to pre-test the idea extensively by getting the crowd to vote on it before you make it. This is what Threadless do with their T-shirt designs. Gustin go one step further. They get members of their user community to pledge to buy their clothing designs before making them.

If you cannot pre-test then be prepared to iterate time and again, taking rejection as a source of feedback and improvement. It is painful but you might just end up with Angry Birds, *Harry Potter* or Google.

THE SEVEN BELLS

A shop in New York is called The Seven Bells, yet it has eight bells hanging outside. Why?

14
Introduce the random

It is not what we don't know that gets us into trouble. It is what we think we know for sure.
MARK TWAIN

A highly effective lateral thinking technique involves the introduction of the random. A random input forces us to start from a new perspective. An excellent way to try this is with the brainstorm method Random word, as described in Exercise B of Appendix 1. Why does a stimulus like the random word work? It forces the brain to start from a new departure point, to come at the problem from a new direction. The brain is a lazy organ; it will automatically lapse into familiar patterns and solve problems the way it has always done unless you give it a jog and start it from a new point. However, the brain is clever at forcing connections between disparate things so when you prompt your mind with a strange stimulus it responds by finding creative connections.

You can also use random pictures, objects, songs or a walk to introduce brainstorm stimuli. You can bring along a selection of photos of random objects or ask people to bring an object that they think will be unusual (without telling them why). You can also ask people to go for a walk in a city centre or around an art gallery or museum and then tell you about something they saw. That then becomes the starting point for the brainstorm.

We tend to mix with the same kinds of people as ourselves; people who will often reinforce our views and opinions. Talking to a random person about a problem can help.

Hans Christian Andersen (1805–1875) was a prolific Danish author who is famed for his fairy tales. Some of his most famous fairy tales include *The Emperor's New Clothes*, *Thumbelina*, *The Snow Queen*, *The Ugly Duckling*, *The Little Mermaid* and *The Princess and the Pea*. They have become popular with children and adults around the world and have inspired plays, films, cartoons and ballets. Andersen was the only child of a shoe maker and a washer-woman. They lived in poverty. His grandfather was assessed as mad and his grandmother worked as a gardener in a lunatic asylum. The young boy often visited her there and conversed with the warders and patients. How random is that? If you mix with people like you, you will hear opinions like yours. Hans Christian Andersen went to a lunatic asylum to hear the wild ramblings of the inmates. They fuelled his imagination. He went on to create ingenious and inspirational fairy stories. Search out different and even random people if you want different and radical ideas.

Welcome the unexpected

We often treat an unexpected, random or surprising happening as an irritation or distraction. It delays us from getting on with the job so we quickly work around it. But sometimes it pays to step back and ponder the meaning of what serendipity has just handed us. Consider these four unexpected occurrences:

1 In 1928 a Scottish bacteriologist returned from his vacation to find that one of his petri dishes had a strange mould growing in it.

2 In the early 1940s a Swiss engineer went for a walk with his dog in the Jura mountains. When he came home he saw that many tiny seed burrs had attached themselves to his trousers and the dog's fur.

3 In 1946 an engineer at Raytheon discovered that a candy in his pocket melted when he worked near an active radar tube.

4 In the 1970s a technician working for a music accessory company wired a circuit incorrectly. The component made a weird moaning sound.

Each of these incidents could have been treated as an annoying accident. Most people might have cleaned the petri dishes, brushed out their trousers, removed the sticky sweet or rewired the circuit correctly. Fortunately for us, the protagonists in these stories all welcomed the unexpected event, investigated and then acted.

1 Sir Alexander Fleming saw that the mould had rejected the bacteria in the dish. He had discovered penicillin – almost by accident. It was a piece of good fortune that led to the development of antibiotics and the saving of millions of lives.

2 George de Mestral examined the burrs under a microscope and saw that they had tiny hooks which caught in the trouser fabric. He went on to develop a new way to fasten materials – Velcro. The word comes from the French words *velours* and *crochet* – a velvet hook.

3 Percy Spencer developed the world's first microwave oven because of this accident.

4 Scott Burnham adapted the strange wail into a guitar pedal sound. He invented the Rat, a pedal that thousands of bands from Nirvana to Radiohead used to enhance their music.

In her 2016 book on the process of invention, *Inventology*, Pagan Kennedy claims that almost half of all inventions started with a serendipitous process. Often this was the result of ideas or discoveries that people had while working on something else.

Kennedy goes on to say that inventors are often polymath connectors 'who by luck or design are able to bring together knowledge from several fields'. She points out that the people most likely to solve problems on the InnoCentive crowdsourcing site are outsiders to the field of the problem.

When something unexpected happens don't get annoyed, get curious. Find out why. The customer with a weird complaint or a weird use for your product is 100 times more interesting than the customer who is happy using your product in a conventional way. Welcome the unexpected.

15
Evaluate

Thinking is the hardest work there is, which is the probable reason why so few engage in it.
HENRY FORD

Harvest the field

There is no use generating a large quantity of ideas if they are not analysed and sifted in order to select those that are worth pursuing. If people participate in creative workshops and then see no follow-up they will lose faith in the process and view the creative workshops as talking sessions only. Once you have generated a large number of ideas you should set about narrowing them down. It is important that you signal this change clearly. You go from the idea generation phase where you are using divergent, creative thinking to the evaluation phase where you use critical and analytical thinking. In the first phase you want as many ideas as possible, but no judgement or criticism is allowed. In the second phase you want to narrow down and select the best ideas by eliminating the many routine or infeasible ones. See Appendix 1 for more guidance on the brainstorming process.

How are you going to select which ideas to carry forward? You need to think about the evaluation criteria you will use before you start the process. Many people choose criteria that are too restrictive; for example, 'We are looking for ideas we can implement this quarter within budget and with no extra resource.' These sorts of criteria probably mean that many good ideas will be filtered out and lost. A very effective selection method recommended by the Synectics groups is to use the NAF criteria. Is the idea Novel, Attractive and Feasible? If it meets these three measures then it is likely to be a good idea.

Tesco use the following criteria for evaluating ideas in their internal suggestions scheme – Better, Simpler, Cheaper. Is this idea better for customers? Is it simpler for staff? Is it cheaper for Tesco?

A consumer goods company uses these criteria for selecting the best ideas for new products – Need, Greed, Succeed, Speed:

Need – is there a real consumer need for this?

Greed – can we make a profit from this?

Succeed – can we build a real winner?

Speed – how soon can we bring this to market?

With the criteria in mind you can start to whittle down the long list into a short list. One way to do this is to perform a triage into good, bad and interesting. Some ideas are obviously good ones and some are obviously bad. But as you go through and cross out the bad ideas, keep asking, 'Could this be adapted or combined with another idea to make it workable?' Third come the 'interesting' ideas – concepts which hold promise but carry severe challenges. They should be mulled over and revisited later as often the very best ideas come from this source.

Another approach is to give everyone a number of votes that they can apply to the list. This saves time when you have a long list of ideas but it means that interesting ideas can be passed over without review. See Appendix 1, Exercise U – Spending £10 – for a fuller description of this approach.

The promising ideas should be analysed further and moved through to a prototype phase as described in the next chapters. The interesting ideas should be kept in a database and allowed to incubate. When you revisit them later you may well find that you now see a way to adapt or combine them into something worthwhile.

We will go on to discuss ways of analysing, evaluating and selecting ideas. De Bono's Six Thinking Hats is a particularly effective way of calmly evaluating, adapting and developing an initially provocative idea. See Appendix 1, Exercise S.

Ways for a group to evaluate a list of ideas:

1 Item by item

Go through the list and perform a triage as described above. Categorize the ideas based on the criteria agreed beforehand, eg NAF – novel, attractive and feasible.

Take multiple passes if necessary. This makes sure that all ideas are reviewed but it can be a long process for a large list.

2 Person by person

Each person in turn says what their favourite ideas are and why they like them. The facilitator ensures that every voice is heard and the choices are recorded. This is fair in that everyone gets a say. It is quicker than a full item-by-item review but one drawback is that later speakers can be influenced by the choices of those who spoke earlier.

3 Everyone at the wall

Everyone goes to the wall where the lists are displayed and puts ticks next to their favourite ideas. This is active and fun. It asks for independent action but does not allow for immediate discussion so it is best to follow up with a review of the favourites.

4 Secret ballot

The ideas are numbered and people write down on separate sheets the numbers of their preferences. The votes are then counted. This is useful in controversial or confrontational situations where people might be afraid to voice their opinions publicly.

(Based on Kaner, 1996)

Evaluation: the gating process

According to the Product Development & Management Association (PDMA) best-practices study, 68 per cent of leading US product developers now use some type of gating process to progress and evaluate innovations from conception of the idea through to full launch of a new product (Cooper, 2002). The general principle is shown in Figure 15.1 in the form of a funnel.

Figure 15.1   The innovation funnel

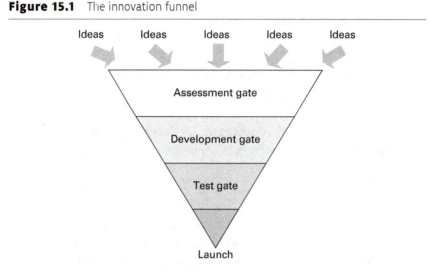

Ideas from all sources flow in at the top of the funnel. They then go through a series of gates. The gating process determines which ideas carry on to the next round and which do not. Typically around two-thirds of the projects fail at each gate. It is sometimes described as a kill or go decision, but the ideas which do not proceed are not killed. They return to the database together with the reasons for the suspension of the idea in case they can be resurrected or recombined with another idea later. The number of gates will be determined by the complexity of the product and the cost of its development. For a small company there may be one or two go/no go decisions. A company like GlaxoSmithKline in pharmaceuticals has around 35 gates in its new product development process. New drugs can take seven years to bring to market – the costs, risks and paybacks are enormous. Sony, on the other hand, launches over 1,000 new products a year. The number of ideas entering the funnel must be truly enormous if over 1,000 make it all the way to launch.

The leading process is Stage-Gate, which is a trademark of Bob Cooper and Scott Edgett. Their methodology is well developed and deployed. Promising new product ideas go through a series of stages and gates. The flow is shown in Figure 15.2.

Figure 15.2 The gating process

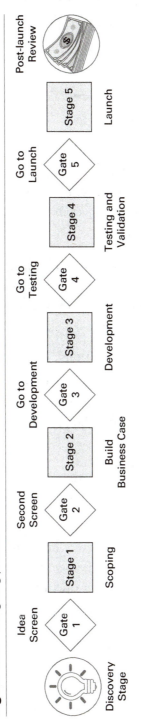

Here is how Cooper describes the five key stages of the process following the discovery or idea generation phase (Product Development Institute, 2002):

- **Stage 1: Scoping**

  A quick and inexpensive assessment of the technical merits of the project and its market prospects.

- **Stage 2: Building the business case**

  This is the critical homework stage – the one that makes or breaks the project. The business case has three main components: product and project definition; project justification; and project plan.

- **Stage 3: Development**

  Business case plans are translated into concrete deliverables. The manufacturing or operations plan is mapped out, the marketing launch and operating plans are developed, and the test plans for the next stage are defined.

- **Stage 4: Testing and validation**

  The purpose of this stage is to provide final and total validation of the entire project: the product itself, the production process, customer acceptance, and the economics of the project.

- **Stage 5: Launch**

  Full commercialization of the product – the beginning of full production and commercial launch.

Each stage involves team activity. A cross-functional team examines the project using key parameters and gathers information in order to make the decision as to whether the project advances to the next stage or not. The team looks at operational, technical, marketing and financial aspects of the proposal to assess potential risk and reward. The proposal has to clear the hurdles in the gate before proceeding to the next stage. Each stage involves more financial commitment and development than the previous stage so at each gate the hurdles are raised. The idea is to kill off those projects that do meet the gating criteria. As projects pass through the gates they are better understood, there is consequently less risk, and more financial and marketing resources can be devoted to them. For a fuller explanation of the process the books and website of Cooper and Edgett are recommended (see References and www.prod-dev.com).

INTERVIEW QUESTION

This question has been used as an aptitude test at interviews. You are driving in your sports car on a cold wet evening. You pass a bus stop where you see three people waiting for the bus. One is your best friend from school days who you have not seen for 20 years. One is the man or woman of your dreams – the person you always wanted to meet. The third is a sick old lady who needs to be taken to hospital. Knowing that there is room for only one passenger in your car, what would you do?

16
Implement

We have to be the change we want in the world.
MAHATMA GANDHI

If all you ever do is think up creative ideas and never try them out then you are not a lateral leader – you are just a wacky thinker. Once you have done a little analysis on a promising idea you should try it out. It is important to avoid 'paralysis by analysis' – the long, drawn-out process of detailed study and an excess of careful evaluation before implementing an initiative. In most situations a pilot study or prototype helps to refine and improve the idea and speeds you towards a successful innovation.

Lateral leaders know that the best way to check out an idea is to try it out. They have a natural inclination for action. They believe that 89 per cent ready and out there now is better than 99 per cent ready and out there too late. Software companies have long had the attitude that it is better to get a 'beta' version of the software out with users in order to get feedback rather than test in-house forever. It is impossible to fully test a product or service in-house because we cannot anticipate exactly how a user will use the product. Lateral leaders do not throw caution and quality to the wind in their search for early testing. They know that it is possible to trade some quality for speed to the market, provided the test is well controlled and in a limited part of the market. They assess the risk and manage it.

Prototyping

Nothing turns a concept into reality faster than a prototype. Before there is a prototype, the idea exists in abstract form only. It is described in words and this leaves scope for misunderstanding. It is hard for the originator to convey exactly what he or she has in mind and it is easy for people to get hold of the wrong end of the stick. Once the prototype exists then people can see, touch and feel the idea. Comments for improvement will flow thick and fast. Whether the prototype is a model in cardboard and string or a software application consisting of a few skeleton screens with nothing behind them, it represents a framework for refinement and extension of the idea.

Great inventors like Edison built thousands of prototypes to test their ideas. James Dyson is an Englishman who invented a new type of vacuum cleaner involving a 'dual cyclone'. He built over 5,000 prototypes as he battled to convince manufacturers and banks to back him. Eventually he got the backing to develop his dream. He produced his first production unit in 1993 and within two years his machine was the market leader in the UK.

Francis Crick and James Watson were researchers at Cambridge University who wrestled with the problem of trying to understand and define the structure of DNA. It was by building models that they were eventually able to visualize the now-famous double helix structure which led to them winning the Nobel Prize in 1962.

1 Analyse but not for long. Think through the idea, plan it and then launch it. Do not undertake massive surveys and market studies. They can be very misleading and the market is changing rapidly. Do not fall into the 'paralysis by analysis' trap where nothing is done for months except studies and spreadsheets.

2 Test market the idea with some key customers or in a chosen region. Do it for real but on a small scale.

3 It is often easier to get permission and budget for a 'pilot' than for a major new initiative, so call it a pilot.

4 Carefully analyse customer reactions and feedback. Adapt and improve the idea.

5 Don't bet the farm on the new idea – even if initial reactions are good. This is the mistake that Marconi plc made in switching entirely out of the defence sector into telecommunications.

6 Always have a fallback plan. If it does not work, cut your losses. Learn the lessons and move on. Don't flog the idea to death trying to force it to work. Try something new.

If we draw a quadrant by plotting ease of implementation of innovations with their level of impact then we can review the options for the four quadrants. The vertical axis represents the degree of difficulty for the organization, from easy to very difficult. The horizontal axis depicts the potential importance of the change, from low impact and low payback to high impact and high payback (and probably high risk). Obviously the exact impact of any innovation is largely unknown at the outset. The benefits have to be estimated on a balance of probabilities. Generally those innovations which are very disruptive are high risk and high reward. But sometimes there are innovations that are high reward and low risk.

In quadrant I we have innovations which are difficult for the organization to implement and which would have a small benefit. It is best to forget these changes and focus on ones with higher paybacks. In quadrant II we have innovations which are easy to implement and have a small impact. These are worth trying on an opportunistic

Figure 16.1 Implementation priorities

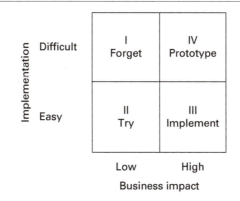

basis. For example, a small change in pricing or customer service levels can sometimes be easy to implement and prove to be profitable. The emphasis here should be on a speedy trial and careful measurement of the impact so that lessons can be learnt quickly.

In quadrant III we have the innovations which are easy to implement and which promise a big payback. These are the best innovations. They should be pursued rigorously but they should nonetheless be planned, implemented and monitored with care. Finally, we arrive at quadrant IV, which involves innovations that promise a lot but are difficult for the organization to implement. These generally involve major changes such as significant cultural changes. A typical example would be a move from a product-based company to a services-based company with a new and untried service offering in the market. These are the kinds of changes that are often avoided because they are risky and frightening. Instead, the board focuses on improving the current methods of the organization or some easy quadrant II-type changes, and shies away from these bigger challenges. But these quadrant IV opportunities are the ones that need to be addressed because they can carry the chance to transform the organization. Often there is a big risk in doing nothing and there are no easy quadrant III options available. Under these circumstances the quadrant IV innovative changes need to be studied carefully and if the promise looks good then they should be tried. Since they are difficult to implement and may represent a major change for the organization, it is best to set up a cross-departmental team to run the pilot and report back. Trying to implement them all across the organization immediately is probably too risky and will generate much opposition.

SINGLE-HANDED

How does a one-armed man change a screw-in light bulb?

17
Welcome failure

It is better to fail in originality than to succeed in imitation.
HERMAN MELVILLE

Fail often to succeed sooner.
TOM KELLEY, IDEO

If you give people the freedom to innovate, the freedom to experiment, the freedom to succeed, then you must also give them the freedom to fail. According to Deepak Seethi of AT&T, the organization of tomorrow will demand mistakes and failures. It is only by trying lots of initiatives that we can improve our chances that one of them will be a star.

In the 1950s the Jacuzzi brothers invented a whirlpool bath to treat people with arthritis. Although the product worked, it was a sales flop. Very few people in the target market, sufferers from arthritis, could afford the expensive bath. So the idea languished until they tried relaunching the same product for a different market – as a luxury item for the wealthy. It became a big success.

What makes Silicon Valley so successful as the engine of high-tech growth? It is the Darwinian process of failure. Commentator and author Mike Malone puts it like this:

> Outsiders think of Silicon Valley as a success, but it is, in truth, a graveyard. Failure is Silicon Valley's greatest strength. Every failed product or enterprise is a lesson stored in the collective memory. We don't stigmatize failure, we admire it. Venture capitalists like to see a little failure in the résumés of entrepreneurs.

Honda Motor Company entered the US market in 1959 with its range of low-powered motorcycles. It endured failure after failure as it learnt the hard way that the little motorcycles popular in the Tokyo suburbs were not well received on the wide open roads of the United States. It eventually brought out a range of high-powered bikes that became very popular. Soichiro Honda, the founder of Honda, said:

> Many people dream of success. Success can only be achieved through repeated failure and introspection. Success represents the 1 per cent of your work that results from the 99 per cent that is called failure. (Cox, 2001: 96)

Accidents will happen – so make the most of them

The greatest of all inventors is accident.
MARK TWAIN

Columbus failed when he set out to find a new route to India. He found America instead (and because he thought it was India he called the natives Indians).

Champagne was invented by a monk called Dom Perignon when a bottle of wine accidentally had a secondary fermentation.

In 1839 Charles Goodyear accidentally dropped some India rubber mixed with sulphur on a hot stove and discovered vulcanization. He obtained a patent for the process in 1844. He capitalized on the accident and the result was a major innovation.

3M invented a glue which was a failure – it did not stick. But it became the basis for the Post-it note, which was a huge success.

Procter & Gamble's Ivory soap was the result of a blunder. A worker left a machine running while he went to lunch. On his return he found that an exceptionally smooth and frothy soap had been formed. He had the initiative to recommend it to the product marketing group who had the sense to seize the opportunity and create a successful new brand based on the accident.

Scientists at Pfizer tested a new drug called Viagra, to relieve high blood pressure. Men in the test group reported that it was a failure as regards high blood pressure but it had one beneficial side effect.

Pfizer, the manufacturers, investigated the side effect and found that the drug had a dramatic effect on men's sexual vigour. Viagra became one of the most successful failures of all time.

In 1978 engineers at Sony Corporation tried to develop a small portable stereo tape recorder. They were unable to do so. They could make it small but they could not make it record, which was one of the design criteria for a tape recorder. The project was written off as a failure. The chairman of Sony was Mr Ibuka, and he had an idea that this failed project could be linked with another Sony project to develop light headphones. He proposed that both products be combined to produce a portable machine that could play tapes through lightweight headphones, and so the Sony Walkman was born. Experts in the industry scoffed at the idea of a tape recorder that could not record and had no speakers, but Sony proved them wrong with an innovative product that was a huge consumer success.

Some of the greatest inventions and discoveries have resulted from a chance, an accident or a failure. The important thing is to have an open-minded attitude, which sees the possibilities in every new piece of knowledge. That way you can seize an opportunity from an accident, as Fleming did.

Even if the failure does not lead directly to a success, it can be seen as a step along the way. Edison's attitude to 'failure' is salutary. When asked why so many of his experiments failed, he explained that they were not failures. Each time he had discovered a method that did not work.

Tom Watson Jr was the legendary president of IBM who led them through the high-growth years when they were the most admired company in America. He encouraged what he called 'wild ducks', people with unconventional and disruptive ideas. On one occasion a vice president who had lost the corporation US $10 million on an experiment that failed was called to Watson's office. The VP was expecting to be fired, so he took his letter of resignation with him and presented it. Watson refused to accept it. 'Why would we want to lose you?' he said. 'We've just given you a US $10 million education.'

Another president who welcomes failure is Richard Branson, founder and head of the Virgin Group. According to his publisher John Brown, 'The secret of his success is his failures. He keeps opening things and a good many of them fail but he doesn't care. He keeps on going.'

In 1985 Coca-Cola experimented by introducing 'New Coke' – a new flavour to replace 'Classic Coke'. It had tested well in consumer tests, but it was a marketing disaster and flopped. Coca-Cola had to eat humble pie and reintroduce Classic Coke. Did this great disaster do any long-term harm to Coca-Cola? Probably not. Did the senior managers and marketing professionals responsible for this failure all get fired? No, they did not. It was an experiment that failed but Coca-Cola survived and grew stronger by it (Ridderstrale and Nordstrom, 1999: 195).

Bill Gates stood down as CEO of Microsoft so that he could focus more time and energy on strategic leadership of the company's development efforts. He took intense interest in Microsoft Research, the 600-person think tank he set up in the early 1990s to push the envelope of software technology, user interface design, speech recognition and computer graphics. As one of his colleagues put it, 'Bill isn't afraid of taking long-term chances. He understands that you have to try everything, because the real secret to innovation is failing fast' (Stein, 2002: 30).

The lateral leader encourages a culture of experimentation. You must teach people that each failure is a step along the road to success. The philosophy of the venture capital funds is salutary. They choose their investments very carefully, but despite their solicitude, for every 10 start-up companies they invest in they expect five to fail, three or four to be modest successes and maybe one or two to be really successful. Those one or two can easily pay back the investment on the portfolio of 10 companies. It is a similar story with business ideas.

Tips for welcoming failure

- Distinguish between two kinds of failure – 'honourable' failure, where an honest attempt at something new or different has been tried unsuccessfully, and 'incompetent' failure, where people fail for lack of effort or competence in standard operations.

- Make sure that staff know that 'honourable' failures will not be criticized.

- Get people to admit to or even boast about failures they have had, where they tried something innovative that did not succeed. Make these into learning experiences.

- In a culture that is very risk averse and keen to apportion blame, tackle the issue head on by rewarding honourable failures. Publicly praise and reward those who have had them.

MATERIAL GAINS

During the Californian gold rush a young entrepreneur went to California with the idea of selling tents to the miners. He thought there would be a good market for tents from the thousands of people who flocked to dig for gold. Unfortunately the weather was so mild that the miners slept in the open air and there was little demand for his tents. What did he do?

18
Use the team

The engine of real economic growth is not technology but innovation.
HECTOR RUIZ, CEO, ADVANCED MICRO DEVICES

There is a strong image of the lone genius – the inspired creative force working alone. But the reality is that teams are generally more effective at generating and refining ideas. In a small team people can spark off each other; an idea from one person can trigger several from others. The great inventor Edison did not create everything himself; he had a team of 14 assistants around him. In his book *The Journey Is the Reward* (1988), Steve Jobs tells how it was the team that created the Apple Macintosh. He recognized their efforts and contributions by casting their signatures on the inside of the casing.

The lateral leader knows how to create a climate of creativity that permeates the whole organization. Every employee feels like an entrepreneur who can contribute ideas and solutions. Every idea, no matter how stupid, is welcomed because it is recognized that bad ideas can help generate good ideas. It is important that senior managers and 'experts' do not criticize new ideas or over-analyse them too quickly. If they show their intellectual superiority by smashing other people's ideas, they turn off the spring which might one day produce a dazzling fountain. You must encourage people to volunteer ideas. A good way to do this is to throw down a challenge to a small team, a department or the whole organization. We have a pressing problem and we need your help to find a good solution. When somebody comes up with an idea which eventually leads to an innovation, they must be recognized, praised and rewarded. Word quickly spreads that good ideas are welcomed, that crazy ideas are not laughed at, and that everyone can contribute to making the organization more successful.

Generic problems that affect everyone can be turned into organization-wide challenges. A good example is finding a new name for the company or for a new product or division. When it comes to more specific challenges, such as designing a new product, then it is generally better to put together a small multi-disciplinary team to crack that one problem. They should own the problem and work on it non-stop through to completion. That way the traditional long lead times involved in getting new products to market can be dramatically shortened.

A major cosmetics company threw down two challenges to its employees. How can we sell more toothpaste? How can we sell more shampoo? Among the answers provided by staff were two that were implemented and made a huge difference. One was to increase the diameter of the hole through which the toothpaste was squeezed so that more toothpaste appeared on the toothbrush. The other was to add the word 'repeat' to the instructions for the shampoo (Cox, 2001: 99).

Google became the leading search engine portal site on the web by innovating. Where does it get its ideas? From its staff, naturally. Google needs a constant stream of new ideas, so it encourages staff in all disciplines to contribute ideas on an internal web page. 'We never say, "This group should innovate and the rest just do their jobs,"' says Jonathan Rosenberg, VP of product management. 'Everyone spends a fraction of their day on R&D.' They found that even employees who would normally be shy about volunteering an idea in a meeting are happy to post one to an intranet page. The best ideas are then discussed at Friday meetings, where individuals get a maximum of 10 minutes to present the most promising ideas. The meeting is kept short and action-oriented. Usually the person who came up with the idea is put in charge of turning it into reality (Warner, 2002a: 52).

The toy giant Mattel enjoyed enormous success with its Barbie brand – a doll for girls that generates over US $2 billion a year in revenue. It wanted to use internal innovations to build on this success. So in 2001, Ivy Ross, then-Senior VP of Girls Toy Design, set up something she called Project Platypus. The idea was based on the description of a platypus as an uncommon mix of different species. The 12 members of the project team were a rotating group drawn from different functions in the company. They joined the project for three months and worked intensely and creatively. Operating in a dramatically different environment, they used external stimuli, studied children at play and had enormous freedom to generate and test ideas. The participants enjoyed the experience and took their new creative skills back to their departments. The results were startling, with many new products and reduced time to market. As Ivy Ross said: 'Designers are not the only people who can create toys. If you put a bunch of creative thinkers in the right environment and drop the job titles, you'll discover amazing creativity' (Salter, 2002: 104).

How should you collect and categorize ideas? Some organizations still use the suggestion box on the cafeteria wall, and this is certainly better than nothing. The up-to-date equivalent is a system based on e-mail or an intranet. Whatever system you use to capture the gush of employee ideas, it is important to categorize them and to respond to them. Every idea must be recorded and evaluated. The originator of the suggestion should receive a note of thanks and be told what will happen next. It is no good encouraging ideas if they are lost or ignored. The ideas should be recorded in a register of ideas, and listed under different categories such as:

- product improvements/extensions;
- safety;
- cost saving;
- staff benefits/welfare;
- processes;
- radical.

Note there is no category for 'bad' or 'silly' ideas. Every idea is welcomed and analysed.

Training

Creativity is not a rare talent possessed only by a handful of gifted individuals. Every one of us can be creative if we are encouraged and shown how to do it. We all have imagination muscles, but many of us have stopped using them. We get so used to the routine of work that we fall into a rut with our thinking. Structured training courses and workshops using techniques such as the ones given later in this book can be used to flex and develop people's creative skills. Just as importantly, these sessions give people the confidence to generate ideas and to be outspoken about change and improvement. With proper training people can develop skills in questioning, brainstorming, adapting, combining, analysing and selecting ideas. They can become the innovative engine your organization needs.

Tips for using the team

- Put together teams from different backgrounds and departments as task forces with specific targets and challenges.

- Ensure the teams are not too large and not too cosy. There should be some constructive tension in the team.

- Select people based on talent, energy, enthusiasm and creative potential and not just on experience and fitness for a task.

- Throw down a challenge to the team. Give them a goal and a time-scale, and make it clear that you expect creative solutions, not just 'more of the same'.

- Drop in on team meetings from time to time to signal their importance and to add a little energy and zest, but do not dominate the meetings or make them your show.

When to go outside: using the external team

Although the internal team is an enormous potential source of ideas, creativity and innovation, it has its limits. It is important to recognize that external input is needed too. This is particularly true if you need to gain insights and ideas from other industries or technologies. A major oil company wanted to reach pockets of oil adjacent to but separate from its main well under the North Sea. It was decided that controlled explosions to blast through would be more effective than drilling. The oil company approached QinetiQ, a research company which had originally been the scientific research arm of the British Ministry of Defence. QinetiQ were experts in bombs and explosives so they were able to help. They also helped a high-performance car manufacturer with the design of their drivers' environment because QinetiQ had experience of cockpit design and instrument layout in fighter planes (Chisholm, 2002).

Most organizations have expertise only in one or two fields, and in the technologies that go with them. So it is essential to look outside for fresh ideas, inputs and techniques. This can be done through a formal process of association with universities, industry bodies and research institutes. The lateral leader should spend time meeting executives from other industries in order to help this process. Directors' associations, chambers of commerce and Rotary clubs are all sources of new contacts and ideas. Executives from commercial companies should spend time with counterparts from the voluntary and public service sectors, and vice versa.

Consultants can be brought in to help stimulate the creative and change process. They have experience from other industries, and they have the advantage of being able to look at your business from an outsider's point of view. They are not ingrained with the assumptions and experiences that imbue you and your colleagues. Some consultants will bring their own sets of assumptions and jump to prescriptive solutions too quickly, but the good ones will ask many searching questions and force you to confront things that you have taken for granted.

Another important external source of ideas is customers. Most companies conduct conventional customer surveys and focus groups. These are useful channels of feedback, but in terms of original ideas they are often disappointing. Customers are good at demanding incremental improvements in products, lower prices and better service, but they are notoriously poor at predicting significant new products or innovations to meet their needs. Before the fax machine was invented, which customers would have predicted they needed it? A more lateral approach to getting insights from customers is to study in detail how they use your type of product or service, and to observe what practical problems they have.

Fluke Corporation of Seattle is noted for innovative hand-held measurement products. They sent teams of observers to watch maintenance engineers in chemical plants, and discovered that the engineers had to carry a variety of different instruments to calibrate different temperature and pressure gauges. They also noticed that after taking the calibration measurement the engineer would write the readings on a clipboard and then transcribe them into a computer. The process was time consuming and prone to errors. Fluke therefore designed a new product that used flexible software to allow it to calibrate any gauge in the chemical plant. It also recorded the results, which could be directly downloaded to the engineer's computer. The resulting product was the Fluke Document Process Calibrator, which became a great success (Cooper and Edgett, 2001).

External sources of input should be drawn on widely, but the ultimate mantle of responsibility for change rests on the shoulders of the senior managers inside the organization. They must draw on external expertise, the creativity of their people, and their own initiatives to drive forward creative ideas into realized innovations. They cannot outsource lateral leadership – they must display it.

Tips for using external sources of ideas

- Recognize that although your internal teams are a great source of ideas you need input from outside as well.
- Identify technologies and processes from outside your field that would be useful.
- Encourage your staff to mix with people from other industries and sectors.
- Formalize external networking by attending cross-industry body meetings and seminars.
- Establish links with local universities and research centres.
- Use consultants sparingly as sources of new insights and ideas.

- Use customers as a source of ideas. Asking them is good but observing them is better.

- Remember that although ideas from outside are good, it is only the ones that are implemented that make a difference, and it is your responsibility to choose and implement them.

GOLDEN GATE

They stopped all traffic on the Golden Gate Bridge in San Francisco, but not due to traffic problems or bridge maintenance. Why do you suppose they did that?

19

Organizing for innovation

Do not go where the path may lead, go instead where there is no path and leave a trail.

RALPH WALDO EMERSON

How should the lateral leader structure the organization to deliver innovation? What management policies should be adopted in order to foster creativity? If the emphasis is on testing out new ideas and prototyping, which part of the company should undertake these functions? Is it better to put fledgling ideas into existing production units, or should they be under the care of a separate innovation unit? The answers depend on the size and nature of the existing business.

The challenge for smaller enterprises

In small businesses, flexibility should be the watchword. The CEO, who may well be the founder, must endeavour to develop an attitude of ownership and an entrepreneurial spirit in every employee. This is more challenging than it sounds. A small company organized around a new product or service has to focus all its energy and time on making the business work. If the idea is successful and demand is strong, production, recruitment, administration, customer service and delivery are all put under pressure as the company grows. On the other hand, if the promising idea is not delivering what was expected, immediate focus is put on fixing what is wrong and on marketing and sales. Cash flow and profitability are weak, so additional funding has to be raised under difficult circumstances. In either set of circumstances there is little bandwidth for innovation. In many ways, the small successful company has the least incentive to innovate, for the managers can see that by executing better and improving processes they can reap the rewards of success. The small enterprise that is struggling should have a powerful motivation to innovate, but instead the natural tendency is to try to fix what is wrong and to bring the existing idea 'back on track'.

Most smaller companies have weekly meetings of the senior managers, where key metrics measuring the progress of the business are reviewed, and where issues are discussed and actions agreed. The focus tends to be on the problems that the business faces. Why is the product not performing to specification? Why are sales behind target? What can we do to improve customer service levels? Why is cash collection behind plan? And so on. Identifying problems and agreeing actions to tackle them are the common currency of management in most business, and these are important activities. However, they leave little or no time for identifying and exploiting new opportunities.

The lateral leader will ensure that time is set aside for opportunity seeking as well as problem solving. The challenge is that today's problems are by their nature pressing and urgent, whereas tomorrow's opportunities are nebulous and unproven. But if all the focus is on fixing today's crop of problems, there is no investment in the seed corn of new ideas which will yield tomorrow's harvest. Radio manufacturers in the United States and Europe in the 1950s were so focused on improving the quality and production of their existing designs of radios based on vacuum tubes (or valves) that they missed the importance of the transistor radio. This left an opportunity for Japanese manufacturers to seize the market with cheaper and more reliable models.

A good policy to overcome this issue is to dedicate one management meeting a month to looking for opportunities, unexpected successes, market trends, competitive actions and new ideas. People will argue that they should not be spending time on this uncertain, blue-sky stuff while the business is threatened with all its current problems, but the leader has to sell the long-term benefits of investing time in these activities alongside the routine, day-to-day fire-fighting.

How the larger enterprise should prepare

It is often assumed that large organizations are slow, lumbering creatures, burdened with bureaucracies and resistant to change. This may be true of some organizations, and is certainly the case with some public service institutions and government agencies. But many large enterprises are well equipped for innovation. Examples of large companies that are leaders in creativity are Apple, Google, Amazon, Tesla Motors, Johnson and Johnson, Procter & Gamble, Microsoft, HP and ABB. These corporations display best practice in innovation management by systematically building it into their processes.

They invite staff to move from one discipline to another so as to break down the silos that can isolate different departments. People are encouraged to move from manufacturing into sales or from research into finance. This is good for morale but even better for developing understanding across departments. It stops sections of the company becoming too rigid and set in their ways. It encourages people to see things from different perspectives.

It is generally thought that diversity, cohesiveness and autonomy will increase the innovation of a team, but research by Sethi, Smith and Park has challenged and refined these ideas (2002: 16). They studied 141 teams developing new product initiatives in consumer products. They found that increased functional diversity on the teams did not necessarily increase innovation. They discovered that high social cohesion between the members of a group could suppress the exchange of views, since cohesive groups focused on maintaining relationships and seeking concurrence. They recommend that managers cut back on the number of functional areas represented on the team, so as to help the team crystallize its identity. They should sprinkle the group with some outsiders so as to lower the social cohesion that can inhibit creativity. Contrary to conventional wisdom, they suggested that senior managers should not adopt a hands-off approach to the group. Close monitoring of the team can motivate them and stress the corporate importance of the project. Finally, they state that expectations of innovation are key. It should be made clear that the team is expected to undertake experimentation and risk taking, rather than incremental improvement of current products and processes.

Successful larger organizations plan for innovation and allocate resources to it in a way that many smaller organizations cannot. They have innovation panels that hold reviews of all their products, services, processes, methods and routes to market. These reviews fulfil the following purposes:

- They identify outmoded and ageing products and processes, and schedule them for replacement. These organizations recognize that everything in business has a life cycle, and the end of a life cycle has to be anticipated so that replacements can be planned. Even systems that are running successfully and profitably today must be examined to see if it is time to replace them with something better. It is much better to make your own products obsolete by introducing superior versions than to find that the competition has beaten you to it.

- They set targets and deadlines in each area and department for the generation of new initiatives in order to replace the items selected as outworn. The general rule is that three new initiatives should be started for each new process needed. A one in three success rate for trials of new products is a good batting average, so it is best to generate a large list of ideas and then whittle down to at least three to be prototyped. Each innovation project should have a project plan, with a deadline for customer feedback and a planned date for a go/no go decision.

- They measure progress against targets for individual projects and for the organization as a whole. They monitor key metrics, including how many new products or processes have been implemented in the last year, what proportion of revenues are coming from new products or services, how many new launches are scheduled for the coming period, and so on. They also try to assess more subjective parameters, such as who is seen as the innovative leader in the industry, and how the organization compares to its competitors in innovation in the marketplace.

- They systematically search for sources of new ideas, from trends in the technology and the industry, from unexpected successes in the marketplace, from customer feedback, and from input from employees at all levels.

- They apply gating processes to projects and prototypes to check that they meet their milestones. They ensure that projects pass marketing, technology and financial hurdles in order to progress and have additional financial and development resources released to them.

Lateral leadership in larger organizations means communicating the importance of innovation in policies and practices as well as in words. So the reward systems recognize that developing new products and processes is of greater value than managing or improving existing well-established products and methods.

Furthermore, it is the best and most promising people who are put into the innovation teams so that these efforts are seen as high value and high prestige. They should be seen as stepping stones to career advancement. The reward system in the innovation teams should be different from existing schemes that reward short-term revenues and contributions. It should treat the team staff as entrepreneurs, and reward them with bonuses for reaching project milestones, and with stock options or other participation in the projects that succeed.

Should innovation prototypes for new businesses, products or services be given to existing departments to manage and develop, or should they put into special incubator units? It is generally much more effective to put them into special units that are focused on innovation. Peter Drucker explains why as follows:

> Innovative efforts should never report to line managers charged with responsibility for ongoing operations. The new project is an infant and will remain one for the foreseeable future, and infants belong in the nursery. Executives in charge of existing businesses or products will have neither the time nor understanding for the infant project. (Drucker, 1985: 149)

This is what IBM did when it had small 'skunkworks' teams compete to develop the personal computer. In just 12 months, Don Estridge and a team of 12 engineers in Boca Raton in Florida built a prototype, gained approval and launched the project that redefined the market and set the new standard for PCs.

Recruiting lateral thinkers

How can you change a corporate culture which is comfortable, complacent and risk averse into one which is dynamic, entrepreneurial and innovative? One key action is to stop hiring comfortable, complacent risk avoiders and start hiring dynamic, entrepreneurial innovators. The trouble is that managers tend to hire people who are like them and who will 'fit in' with the team. And the people who will fit in with a conventional, unadventurous team will probably have conventional, unadventurous views and attitudes.

Many managers who have a young team would be reluctant to add an older member or someone from a completely different background because of the fear that they might not fit in. But homogeneous teams are less effective than diverse ones. Studies show that teams that get on well together are less creative than teams where there is some contention. If people in a group nearly always agree with each other then they are operating within their comfort zones. If you want more creative ideas and more innovation in your organization then you need to hire people who will think differently and challenge orthodox policies. Hiring managers should be told to avoid the natural inclination to hire people who will fit in and where possible to hire people with diverse backgrounds and people who display creative potential.

How can you spot lateral thinkers, innovators and entrepreneurs? Here are some questions that you can ask at interview which might help.

- **How do you like to be managed?**

  Do you like a boss who gives you lots of close support or one who lets you get on with it? Entrepreneurs like clear objectives and plenty of freedom in how to go about their work.

- **What are your main hobbies outside of work?**

  What is fun for you? This type of question sheds light on how creative they are. Creative people do creative things outside of work. Someone who plays in a band, writes blogs or paints is more likely to be a lateral thinker than someone who enjoys watching TV, playing golf or going out with friends.

- **Tell me about a time that you took the initiative and solved a problem at work creatively**

  Do not take their answer at face value but ask some follow-up questions to see just what their contribution really was.

- **Tell me about a time when you took a risk that failed**

  Creative entrepreneurial people are comfortable taking risks. They accept that failure is part of the process and they learn from it. Someone who has never failed has never tried anything new or adventurous.

- **How would you approach this kind of problem that we might have here?**

  Give them a real or hypothetical question relating to a tough challenge that you could face. They should not give you a pat answer but should ask some questions and provide some possible ideas. You are testing their problem-solving approach.

You can also try a problem that is unrelated to the job just to see how they think. For example, 'Can you think of any creative ideas to reduce traffic congestion in this city?' There is no right answer here but there are plenty of safe predictable options. However, the lateral thinker is likely to come up with some unorthodox approaches.

Another good indicator at the interview is the type of question they ask you. Offer the candidate the opportunity to ask questions. Do they ask detail-oriented, mundane questions or bigger picture, strategic questions?

If you want more innovation then you do not want a team of lookalikes who think alike. You want a mix of skills, experiences, backgrounds and attitudes. All the team members should buy into the values, vision and goals for the organization, but if they have lots of different views about how best to achieve the goals then so much the better. Let's welcome all those ideas, select the best ones and try them.

Measuring creativity

Can creativity be measured? Can an organization establish metrics to calibrate its innovative capabilities? Creativity is to some extent subjective. It is hard to measure in an absolute sense, but metrics can be put in place to give an estimate of how well your organization is doing and whether you are getting better or worse. The innovation test questionnaire in Chapter 3 is one example. Furthermore, you can establish measures for people, processes and products to estimate creativity and innovation.

Managers can assess their team members for creativity in terms of originality of work, ideas and suggestions made, open mindedness, receptivity to ideas from outside and so on. Employees should be appraised in this regard and the assessment discussed with them in an open fashion. Areas for improvement can be identified and action plans – such as training – put in place.

All internal processes can be reviewed and assessed in the light of these questions:

- Has this process been improved or streamlined in the last year?
- How many new processes have we implemented to replace outmoded or irrelevant ones?

Similarly for products and services:

- How many new products or services have we brought to market in the last year?
- What proportion of our total revenue comes from products or services which were launched within the last two years? The average figure for companies across the EU is 20 per cent.
- How long does it take between the initial approval of an idea for a new product and its launch?
- What proportion of our capital investment is spent on new product development?
- Are we reaching our targets for new product development and launch?

- How does our R&D investment compare with our competitors, and how does our output of new products, initiatives and patents compare with the industry standard?

- Are we seen in the industry as a product and service innovator?

In order to answer the last question and others like it, we might conduct surveys among customers, suppliers and employees to assess how we are perceived in innovation, receptiveness to change and originality.

Another area where we should endeavour to measure and reward innovation is in the employee appraisal process. This is typically a yearly event where employees assess their performances against objectives, and following a discussion the manager gives an appraisal rating. The following types of question can be added to the self-assessment form:

- What ideas have you generated and championed this year?

- What innovations have you implemented in your work?

Just by adding these questions, managers send a powerful signal that innovation and creativity are valued and measured.

Tips for organizing for innovation

- Hold meetings that are focused on opportunities rather than problems.

- Communicate the benefits to the whole organization of investing in innovation.

- Set targets for innovation in products, services and processes.

- Identify existing products and processes that are scheduled for retirement.

- Target three new initiatives for every innovation needed.

- Set up cross-functional teams with clear innovation objectives, and motivate them to be radical and take risks.

- Put prototype implementation into a separate department or function (the 'innovation incubator') staffed by go-getters who have a good diversity of skills.

- Set goals and deadlines.
- Implement a gating procedure to evaluate ideas and prototypes using a system such as Stage-Gate (a trademark of R G Cooper and associates).
- Measure innovation performance for people, products and processes against targets.
- Put someone with clout and prestige in charge of innovation efforts.
- Encourage people to move laterally within the organization from department to department to cross-fertilize ideas and cultures.
- Put your best people on innovation projects, and ensure that such projects are seen as good for career development.

LATE TRAIN

A businessman called the train station to find the time of his train but when he reached the station he was surprised to learn that he was half an hour early. What time was his train?

20
Common mistakes: 12 great ways to crush creativity

He shows great originality, which must be curbed at all costs.
SCHOOL REPORT ON THE ACTOR PETER USTINOV

If the lateral leader is doing all the right things, entrepreneurial spirit will flow through the organization, generating a stream of ideas which result in innovation. So why is it not happening? Most CEOs, chairpersons, VPs and directors recognize that their organizations need to improve creativity and bring forward a flow of innovative goods and services. Yet they do not put in place training or processes to make this happen. Worse still, they may be unaware that many practices in their operations inhibit ideas and strangle innovation at birth. Here are some of the most common mistakes, and all of them are great ways to crush creativity (based on Sloane, 2002).

Criticism

A natural reaction to any new idea you hear is to criticize it, to point out some of the weaknesses and flaws that will hold it back. The more experienced you are and the more intelligent you are, the easier it is to find fault with other people's ideas. Decca Records turned down the Beatles, IBM rejected the photocopying idea that launched Xerox, DEC turned down the spreadsheet and various major publishers turned down the first *Harry Potter* novel. The same thing is happening in most organizations today. New ideas tend to be partly formed and not fully thought through, so it is easy to reject them as 'bad'. They diverge from the narrow focus that we have for the business, so we put them to one side. But there is no such thing as a 'bad' idea. Bad ideas are often excellent springboards for good ideas. Every organization needs lots of bad, silly, stupid, crazy ideas, because within them there are concepts we can adapt to make into workable innovations.

What is more, every time somebody comes to you with an idea that you criticize, it discourages the person from making any more suggestions. It sends a message that new ideas are not welcome, and that anyone who volunteers them is risking criticism or ridicule. This is a sure way to crush the creative spirit in your staff.

Neglecting brainstorms

Brainstorming is seen by some as old-fashioned and passé, but good brainstorms remain one of the best ways of generating fresh ideas and involving staff from all levels. If your organization is not holding frequent brainstorming sessions to find creative solutions, you are missing a great opportunity for new ideas and sending a message to staff that their input is not required. Your brainstorming sessions should be short and have a high energy level. They should have a clear focus and generate a large number of ideas. They should be chaired by an enthusiastic facilitator who encourages the flow and ensures that there is no initial criticism or judgement of the ideas.

Problem hoarding

There is a macho concept that directors and senior managers should shoulder the responsibility for solving all the company's major problems. Strategic issues are too complicated and high level for the ordinary staff. There is a fear that if people at the grass roots knew some of the strategic challenges the organization faces, they would feel insecure and threatened. But people lower down the organization are often closer to the customer, and they can see what is working and what isn't. They have a pretty shrewd notion of what is going on. If you involve them and throw down a challenge to help find solutions, you will find a rich source of new ideas and a shared sense of purpose. You will get better decisions, and the staff are much more likely to buy into initiatives that they have helped form than to accept things handed down.

Efficiency over innovation

It is natural for managers to focus on making the current business model work better. Every process can be improved. But if we focus entirely on making things better, we can miss the chance to make things different, and that is the essence of innovation. Ultimately innovation beats efficiency. If you were making slide rules, improving efficiency would not have stopped electronic calculators wiping you out. You have to improve the current process while continually looking for and trying out new methods of delivering value to customers. An exclusive focus on efficiency is a dangerous blinker.

Overworking

Often allied to the focus on efficiency is a culture of long hours and hard work. The problem here is the belief that hard work alone will solve the problem. Often we need to find a different way of solving a problem rather than just to work harder at the old way of doing things. We need to take time to look for new opportunities. If you are focused on one way of doing things and working all hours to make it happen, how can you find time to try new ways of reaching your goals? If you had been making gas lamps and you worked all day to produce more lamps, you would have had no time to learn about electricity and develop an electric light. Our working day needs time for some fun, some lateral thinking, some wild ideas and some testing of new initiatives.

It isn't in the plan

'We cannot try that idea because it is not in the plan and we have no budget for it.' Organizations that plan in great detail and then adhere to those plans are placing themselves in a straitjacket. They are limiting themselves to a vision of the world as the planners saw it when they conceived the plan. Markets and needs change so quickly that the view we had last week can be out of date today. So how accurate can the plan we did last December be? Corporate plans should be loose frameworks to be used as guidelines rather than detailed route maps. They must allow for sudden changes in market conditions, new threats and opportunities, and for experimentation. The plan should not become a bunker within which unimaginative managers can hide.

Laying the blame

A culture of blame for failure is a sure-fire way to halt entrepreneurial spirit in its tracks. Most innovation projects will fail, but they are still worthwhile because it is only by trying them that you can determine which promising ideas are duds and which are winners. If people fear that they will be blamed for failing, why should they try something new?

Wrong rewards

If your bonuses are structured to reward well-established products and businesses, chances are they are completely wrong for starting new business lines. Typical bonuses give percentages of quarterly revenues and contribution as rewards for success. But for its first few quarters a new product or service may yield little revenue and negative contribution. You need different incentives for the team running an innovation project. They should be rewarded for reaching agreed milestones. They should be treated as entrepreneurs and given stock options linked to the longer-term success of their project.

Outsourcing change

Consultants can provide many useful skills, and one of them is looking at your business as an outsider who is not bound by the assumptions and beliefs that you hold. They can help you see things that should have been obvious. But the risk is that if you hand over all responsibility for conceiving and implementing new methods, products or processes to external consultants, very few people in the organization feel ownership. There can be a sense of resentment and pushback against other people's ideas. The trick is to use the consultants as catalysts and spurs to innovation, but to involve many staff early in the project to get their ideas and input. The front-line staff are closer to the customer and closer to the action than senior managers or consultants, and they can help shape ideas to make them more workable. They will also be much more committed to making the change a success if they helped to design it.

Promotion from within

Promoting from within is generally a good sign. It helps retain good people, and staff can see a reward for loyalty and hard work. However, if all the managers are promoted from within, it means they have all grown up in the same culture. It is harder for them to see the flaws and weaknesses in your processes. It is harder for them to view the business with an outsider's eyes. You can end up with a 'this is how we do things here' attitude – resistant to change and disruptive ideas. Some fresh blood in the management team will help you to see other ways to do things. When you recruit, do not just look for people who will 'fit in' and conform to the corporate mould. Look for people who are different and can dare to bring heretical views into the organization.

Giving innovation projects to production units

A common mistake in larger organizations is to give innovation projects to existing line managers who are running the regular business as well. It can seem a natural thing to do, but it is generally fatal. New products or services are like delicate seedlings that should be kept in the greenhouse until they are stronger, and not left to fend for themselves. The regular business manager is too busy meeting monthly deadlines and targets to give the prototype business the attention it needs. It is better to put the seedlings in the care of a special department, sometimes known as an innovation incubator. This department has different goals and objectives, it works to a longer schedule, and it is headed by an innovation director who has a high level of authority in the organization.

No training

Every one of us can be more creative if we are encouraged and shown how to do it. We were all imaginative as children, but gradually most people have their creative instincts ground down by the routine of work. With proper training, people can develop skills in questioning, brainstorming, adapting, combining, analysing and selecting ideas. They can rediscover their imaginations.

EASYJET

easyJet is a leading low-cost air carrier in Europe. It has been responsible for many innovations in low-cost air travel. There are no free drinks on easyJet flights. If you want a drink you have to buy it. According to a recent magazine article there are two major business benefits from this policy. One is the income generated. What do you think is the second?

21 great ways to innovate

The lateral leader is always looking for new ways to innovate. Continuous innovation is not easy and if you keep using the same method you will experience diminishing results. How can you repeatedly implement great new products, processes or services? Try innovating how you innovate by employing some of these ideas.

1 Copy someone else's idea

One of the best ways to innovate is to pinch an idea that works elsewhere and apply it in your business. Henry Ford saw the production line working in a meat packing plant and then applied to the automobile industry, thereby dramatically reducing assembly times and costs.

2 Ask customers

If you simply ask your customers how you could improve your product or service they will give you plenty of ideas for incremental innovations. Typically they will ask for new features or that you make your product cheaper, faster, easier to use, available in different styles and colours etc. Listen to these requests carefully and choose the ones that will really pay back.

3 Observe customers

Do not just ask them, watch them. Try to see how customers use your products. Do they use them in new ways? This was what Levi Strauss saw when they found that customers ripped the jeans – so they brought out a line of pre-ripped jeans. Heinz noticed that people stored their sauce jars upside down so they designed an upside-down bottle.

4 Use difficulties and complaints

If customers have difficulties with any aspect of using your product or if they register complaints, then you have a strong starting point for innovations. Make your product easier to use, eliminate the current inconveniences and introduce improvements that overcome the complaints.

5 Combine

Combine your product with something else to make something new. It works at all levels. Think of a suitcase with wheels, or a mobile phone with a camera or a flight with a massage.

6 Eliminate

What could you take out of your product or service to make it better? The Sony Walkman eliminated speakers and recording functions, Ryanair eliminated the use of travel agents and printed tickets, Tesla Motors eliminated dealer showrooms and petrol engines.

7 Ask your staff

Challenge the people who work in the business to find new and better ways to do things and new and better ways to please customers. They are close to the action and can see opportunities for innovation. Often they just need encouragement to bring forward great ideas.

8 Plan

Include targets for new products and services in your business plan. Put it onto the balanced scorecard. Write innovation into everyone's objectives. Measure it and it will happen.

9 Run brainstorms

Have regular brainstorm meetings where you generate a large quantity of new product ideas. Use diverse groups from different areas of the business and include a provocative outsider, eg a customer or supplier.

10 Examine patents

Check through patents that apply in your field. Are there some that you could license? Are some expiring so that you can now use that method? Is there a different way of achieving the essential idea in a patent?

11 Collaborate

Work with another company who can take you to places you can't go. Choose a partner with a similar philosophy but different skills. That is what Mercedes did with Swatch when they came up with the SMART car.

12 Minimize or maximize

Take something that is standard in the industry and minimize or maximize it. Ryanair minimized price and customer service. Starbucks maximized price and customer experience. It is better to be different than to be better.

13 Run a contest

Ask members of the public to suggest great new product ideas. Offer a prize. Give people a clear, focused goal and they will surprise you with novel ideas. This is good for innovation and PR.

14 Ask – what if?

Do some lateral thinking by asking what if…? Challenge every boundary and assumption that applies in your field. You and your group will come up with amazing ideas once the normal constraints are lifted.

15 Watch the competition

Do not slavishly follow the competition but watch them intelligently. The small guys are often the most innovative so see if you can adapt or license one of their ideas – or even buy the company!

16 Outsource

Subcontract your new product development challenge to a design company, a university, a start-up or a crowdsourcing site like InnoCentive or NineSigma.

17 Use open innovation

Big consumer products companies like Procter & Gamble or Reckitt Benckiser encourage developers to bring novel products to them. They are flexible on IP protection and give a clear focus on what they are looking for. A large proportion of their new products now start life outside the company.

18 Adapt a product to a new use

Find an entirely different application for an existing product. De Beers produced industrial diamonds but found a new use for diamonds when they introduced the concept of engagement rings. It opened up a large new market for them.

19 Try Triz

Triz is a systematic method for solving problems. It can be applied in many fields but is particularly useful in engineering and product design. Triz gives you a toolbox of methods to solve contradictions, for example 'how can we make this product run faster but with less power?'

20 Go back in time

Look back at methods and services that were used in your sector years ago but have now fallen out of use. Can you bring one back in a new updated form? It has been said that speed dating is really a relaunch of a Victorian dance format where ladies had cards marked with appointments.

21 Use social networks

Follow trends and ask questions on platforms like Twitter or Facebook. Ask what people want to see in future products or what the big new idea will be. Many early adopters are active on social network groups and will happily respond with suggestions.

The ways to innovate are legion. Try some approaches that are new to you in order to boost your innovation capability.

22
Summary

It should be borne in mind that there is nothing more difficult to handle, more doubtful of success and more dangerous to carry through than initiating changes. The innovator makes enemies of all those who prospered under the old order and receives only lukewarm support from those who would prosper under the new.
NICCOLÒ MACHIAVELLI

The lateral leader understands the need to change the spirit of the organization to one where everyone has a creative and entrepreneurial approach to problem solving. To do this you need to develop lateral leadership traits and techniques in order to inspire and coach your people to fulfil their creative potential. The three building blocks are:

- the vision;
- the culture;
- the process.

The lateral leader spends enormous time and effort communicating the vision and the messages that derive from it. Every means of communication is pressed into use in order to facilitate a two-way flow of traffic. The leader communicates the direction and objectives, and listens carefully to the concerns, ideas and feedback from all levels so as to adapt plans and transfer creativity, knowledge and best practice.

It takes an extended period to change a corporate culture, and it is one of the CEO's most challenging assignments. But it is essential to generate a single unifying corporate culture that embodies these attributes:

- openness to ideas and input;
- questioning of authority and conventional wisdom;

- agility – ready, willing and able to change quickly;
- goal achievement oriented;
- entrepreneurial spirit at all levels;
- ready to take risks and learn from failure.

The third element is the building of a process for innovation. It is not something bolted on at monthly management meetings – it becomes an integral part of the whole business. Innovation targets and measurements are set. There are clear goals for the number of new products, processes, alliances and so on that are needed, together with deadlines for their delivery. Cross-functional teams are set up to tackle important assignments. Lateral thinking and creativity techniques are taught and used for questioning assumptions, taking new views on the business, and adapting and combining ideas from other sources. Everyone's ideas and input are welcomed.

No idea is a bad idea, but ideas on their own are not enough. It is by carefully selecting the best ideas and then prototyping them that creativity can be turned into innovation. In larger organizations there may well be a special innovation department under a VP of innovation who oversees the trials of dozens of promising concepts. They are quickly tested in the marketplace so that real customer reaction can be gauged and the idea adapted or dropped. Many innovations will fail, and lessons are learnt from them. The company heavily backs those that succeed, and they are rapidly rolled out into full production with all the systems, marketing and structural support that are needed.

The magic sentence

The easiest way to crush creativity is to find fault with new ideas that colleagues or subordinates bring forward. The more clever and more experienced you are, the easier it is to shoot holes in any proposal. You can show your superior intelligence and highly honed management analysis skills by listing all the flaws in their arguments. As all the experts pointed out to Marconi, radio waves travel in straight lines and the Earth is a sphere, so it is silly to think of transmitting a

Figure 22.1 The building blocks of success

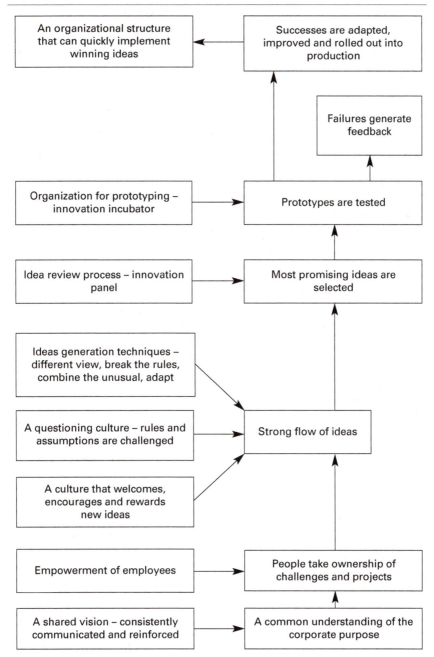

radio signal across the Atlantic. All it takes is for a few crazy ideas to be shot down, and people stop volunteering them.

So the next time someone comes to you with a wacky, half-formed idea that you can immediately see is riddled with faults, bite your tongue and say the following:

That sounds interesting. How can we make it work?

Then let the person talk. As he or she expands on the idea, you will almost certainly see ways in which it could be adapted to work. Explore it constructively together and you stand a better chance of coming up with a winner. What is more, the person who was courageous enough to suggest the idea feels motivated to improve on it, and encouraged to come up with more in the future.

An atmosphere where ideas are criticized will crush creativity and deter people from coming forward. An atmosphere that welcomes ideas is a necessary prerequisite for an innovative organization. It is an essential foundation on which to build an entrepreneurial enterprise. The building blocks of success are shown in Figure 22.1.

Checklist

This is your summary checklist for using the principles of the lateral leader to transform your organization into an innovation engine:

1   Recognize and communicate the need for change.

2   Paint the goal. Achieve a shared vision among all the staff of what the destination looks like. Reinforce the vision in all communication.

3   Empower employees to find their own ways to make the vision a reality. Give them the information, motivation and freedom to do this individually and in groups.

4   Plan for change and prepare for setbacks along the way.

5   Stay focused on the goal despite day-to-day distractions.

6   Use innovation techniques and exercises to develop the skills of your people.

7 Check your assumptions in every situation. Test what boundaries and unwritten rules are constraining you.

8 Ask searching questions to get to the bottom of issues. Encourage a climate of questioning where every business rule and assumption can be challenged by anyone.

9 Deliberately adopt a different point of view. Force yourself to approach issues from new directions.

10 Combine the unusual. Try putting together crazy mixtures in order to create new products, services or concepts.

11 Search for ideas in other industries or areas that you can adapt for your business.

12 Change the rules of the game in order to outflank your competitors.

13 Generate a great many ideas before selecting a way forward. One good idea is not enough – you need many in order to select the best.

14 Test ideas in small ways. Create prototypes. Observe customer reactions. Adapt and develop.

15 Welcome failure as a stepping stone to success. Make sure that your people know they will not be punished for good endeavours that do not succeed.

16 Use the team. Throw down a challenge to your staff and encourage them to generate innovative ideas. Then back them to deliver solutions.

17 Set goals and metrics for innovation. Measure progress against the goals for individual projects and for the organization as a whole.

18 In larger organizations have separate 'innovation incubators' headed by someone with power and prestige. Staff them with your best people and reward them as entrepreneurs.

19 Gather all ideas in a register of ideas, typically on an extranet. Categorize, analyse and feed back to contributors.

20 Set up a gating process to evaluate prototypes so that they have to clear hurdles to survive and earn more funding.

Lateral leadership in action

Lateral leadership is all about inspiring and motivating the team, and thereby equipping and enabling the organization to be more agile, more responsive to change and more innovative. It starts with a shared vision, develops through effective communication, and delivers by empowering staff to be creative and entrepreneurial. But the team needs more than exhortation and mission statements. Creative principles, lateral thinking techniques and targeted training are all needed to make the transformation of the organization from dozing dullard to innovation champion.

It is a long path, and people's skills and confidence have to be developed and encouraged. At each stage, lateral leaders have to show through their actions that they are creative, they welcome creativity, and they are focused on reaching the goals. That is why they will check their assumptions, ask searching questions, deliberately adopt a different point of view, adapt or combine ideas, and try out new initiatives. They will gradually shape the culture of the organization to be more questioning and entrepreneurial. They will put in place structures, policies and an organization that can take new ideas and analyse, assess and select the best. The selected ideas are prototyped and nurtured in special departments. Above all, lateral leaders will show that they believe in their people and trust them to take risks. Everyone needs help if they are to seize opportunities, think creatively, take entrepreneurial risks and become lateral leaders themselves.

23
The lateral leadership course

Problems are just opportunities in their work clothes.
HENRY KAISER

How can an individual manager or team of managers acquire the characteristics and skills of the lateral leader? Some traits of the lateral leader come naturally to certain people, whereas others find them difficult to acquire. However, if you buy into the benefits of a lateral leadership style, it is possible for you to change your actions and behaviour to become more of a lateral leader than you are today. The recommended initial action is a two-day off-site workshop – the lateral leadership course. It can be crammed into one day, but then it tends to be rushed. Some teams will need three days, particularly if the vision and strategic objectives are not already agreed and have to be hammered out during the course. The objectives of this workshop are to:

1 agree the vision, goals and strategic direction (if this has not already been done);

2 set a common agenda for change and for lateral leadership;

3 set creativity goals and metrics;

4 develop skills in questioning, challenging assumptions, creative problem solving, idea generation, idea analysis and evaluation;

5 agree action plans to implement a lateral leadership programme throughout the organization;

6 have fun and build team spirit along the way.

The participants

Ideally the first people to go on the course are the CEO and his or her senior team – maybe six to eight people in total. This is followed by other courses for senior managers so that a new common vision, purpose and behaviour model are shared. It is important that the participants buy into the goals and philosophy of the course before they attend. They need to bring an attitude that is receptive to change and to acquiring new skills. Obviously there should be no distractions during the course, so it is better held off-site. Getting the senior people to leave their day-to-day tasks and mobile phones behind is a tough challenge. If it is not faced there is a real danger that the course will be undermined, as they will spend much of the time talking to each other about current issues, fire fights and turf wars, reading e-mails or talking to the office. It is therefore essential as a preliminary that there is a shared purpose of what is to be achieved on the workshop and of its importance.

In addition to the participants there is a facilitator who understands the culture and nature of the company. The facilitator will:

- lead the group through the various phases;
- encourage their full participation;
- guide them through the difficult parts;
- motivate them to believe in their own creative potential;
- challenge them to achieve more than they thought possible;
- teach them about lateral leadership;
- develop their creative and leadership skills.

Phase I: Introductions

People should get to know each other. Expectations from the course should be shared. The agenda is presented and discussed. An icebreaker of some kind may be appropriate to get people relaxed and open-minded.

Phase II: Brainstorming to start the flow

Once the energy level has been raised it is time to get the creative juices flowing. Brainstorming is a good way to start this process. Exercises A, B, C, D and E in Appendix 1 are excellent tools to use at this stage of the workshop. Spending 60 to 90 minutes on this phase will pay back, because the delegates will learn fresh skills on brainstorming, including the use of variants like Random word, Restate the problem and Reverse the problem. They can use these skills in later stages of the workshop. The problems to be solved should be general rather than specific to the organization. Typical topics that can be used for the exercises are:

- How can we get everyone to use public transport?
- How could we win all the gold medals at the next Olympic Games?
- How can we get everyone to take more exercise?
- How can we persuade young people not to start smoking?
- How could you double the sales of your local flower shop?

The facilitator encourages all the participants to contribute, and rigorously enforces the rule about no early judgement or criticism of ideas.

Phase III: The vision and its components

The vision may already be understood and agreed; if so, this phase can be skipped. If it is not, a key part of the workshop is to define it. There are various well-established methods and approaches to setting the vision, and indeed it is a topic worthy of a book and a workshop all its own. The facilitator leads a discussion, using creative techniques to define the vision. Our preferred approach is to start by examining four elements that underpin the vision:

- a purpose;
- a mission;
- a culture;
- a set of values.

The purpose is the fundamental reason for the organization's existence. To define this you need to ask at the most basic level, 'Why do we exist and what is it we do?' The Coca-Cola purpose is expressed in what they call their promise:

> The Coca-Cola Company exists to benefit and refresh everyone who is touched by our business.

The mission is a forward-looking expression of the purpose of the company. It should inspire and challenge without being too prescriptive. So the Coca-Cola mission is:

> When we bring refreshment, value, joy and fun to our stakeholders, then we successfully nurture and protect our brands, particularly Coca-Cola. That is the key to fulfilling our ultimate obligation to provide consistently attractive returns to the owners of our business.

The Ford mission statement is:

> We are a global family with a proud heritage, passionately committed to providing personal mobility for people around the world. We anticipate consumer needs and deliver outstanding products and services that improve people's lives.

This feeds into their vision, which is:

> To become the world's leading consumer company for automotive products and services.

The Microsoft mission is:

> To enable people and businesses throughout the world to realize their full potential.

The mission should be simple, clear and meaningful to staff and customers alike.

The corporate culture expresses the style and manner in which the company operates. So the culture statement generally makes great play of employee empowerment, development, challenge and so on. Adjectives such as innovative, enthusiastic, dynamic, energetic, customer-focused, learning, decentralized and empowered are often used. Unfortunately, the cultures that the directors list are often some distance from the reality in the organization. The culture statement should not be a series of platitudes or a wish list for the future. You should spend time in a workshop session defining as much about the current corporate structure as you can – strengths and weaknesses. Then look realistically at how the culture could be strengthened and developed. The resulting culture statement should be rooted in reality, but with sensible goals for improvement.

Similarly with the values; if the current values are to cut costs and maximize profitability, it is no good mouthing pious declarations about customer service, employee development and environmental responsibility. The workshop is a good place to take a hard look at the current corporate values and to build on the good ones. The values statement should be a summary of what the organization really stands for, what it believes in and aspires to.

Finally, the vision is a short statement that encapsulates the essence of the culture, values, purpose and mission. The four components underpin the vision, but the vision cannot simply amalgamate all the previous statements, or it becomes unwieldy and impractical. Brevity in vision statements is a great benefit. Microsoft's vision is:

> Empowering people through great software – any time, any place and on any device.

If time allows, the group should examine each of the four components of the vision, using creative questioning approaches and techniques such as six thinking hats (de Bono, 1985) to analyse and evaluate different options. Finally, the vision statement itself should be discussed and agreed. It is also possible to start with the vision and then analyse the four components subsequently. Either way it is important to agree a statement that is succinct and has a strong sense of purpose and direction. It will be the platform for the strategy and change objectives that follow.

Figure 23.1   The Ikea vision

Figure 23.2   Tesla's mission

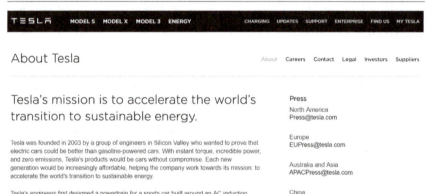

Phase IV: Creative exercises

It is a good idea to intersperse creative leadership exercises with specific business-oriented activities. The variety helps stimulate the brain, and the lessons learnt from the exercises can immediately be put to use on the business tasks. So Phase IV consists of creative exercises. The facilitator will choose one or two of the following exercises from Appendix 1 – the choice depends on timing and suitability for the group.

Exercise F – Break the rules.

Exercise G – The worst solution.

Exercise H – Idea cards.

Exercise I – Found objects.

Phase V: Strategy, goals and objectives

Once the vision is firmly agreed, the facilitator leads the group to review the strategic objectives. It is very important at this stage that the team discards all assumptions about the business and how it operates, and instead everyone thinks laterally about different ways in which the vision can be realized. There are numerous ways to approach this challenge. Our recommended method is to go through the following stages.

Past, present and future

The team analyses what the industry or market looked like three years ago, what it looks like today and what it will look like in three years' time. This covers topics like technologies, routes to market, key customer requirements and priorities, competitive characteristics, pricing and products. If you list the parameters down the side and the three time frames across the top, it is possible to build a picture of the trends that are affecting the industry. In this exercise you are trying to view the market as a video rather than a snapshot.

SWOT analysis

The team analyses the strengths, weaknesses, opportunities and threats facing the organization. This should be a familiar exercise to most business people. It is a critical review of the company's position in the market. Participants are usually accurate in their assessment of the strengths and weaknesses of the organization, but they do not think widely enough in the opportunities and threats categories. A threat is anything that can undermine your market position or take customers away. For example, videoconferencing over the internet is a threat to airlines, because businessmen and women might prefer to videoconference with a remote client rather than fly to visit them. Similarly with opportunities; who would have thought there was an opportunity for Virgin Group to go into trains or cola drinks? The facilitator should use creative techniques to stretch the imaginations of the participants and encourage them to think outside their normal boundaries.

PEST analysis

If appropriate the team can analyse the political, economic, social and technological factors that could influence the business over the next five years. The sorts of questions that are raised are:

- What if the price of oil were to double?
- What if there was a revolution in our major overseas market?
- What if there was a change of government and policy in key areas?
- What are the demographic changes affecting our customers?
- What could threaten or change the technology that our products use?
- What if fashions changed radically?
- What if interest rates were to double or treble?

Scenario planning

The SWOT and PEST analyses lead directly into scenario planning, where two or three starkly different scenarios are drawn, and the team brainstorms strategies to handle them. Typically, one scenario would be a very difficult outlook with factors such as worsening economic conditions, increased competition and downward price movements. A second scenario might be more benign market conditions. A third might be a radical shift in the environment in which the organization operates, with new technologies and new ways to reach customers.

Each scenario is brainstormed, and radical approaches are sought to maximize the organization's performance in each case. By looking at different possible futures for the business, the participants can develop a range of new ideas and strategies for consideration.

Strategies, goals and objectives

From the preceding exercises the team can now draw together the agreed strategies and strategic goals for the organization. These should be bold, challenging but realistic. They will include financial targets and objectives for markets, customers, operations and staffing. Time should then be spent cascading these strategic goals down into departmental goals and objectives.

Innovation metrics

One of the sets of objectives that should be defined is the list of innovation objectives. This should support the strategic objectives and define targets such as:

- the number of new products;
- revenue from new products in existing markets;
- revenue from new markets or ventures;
- the number of new strategic partnerships;
- the areas where new processes or procedures will be implemented;
- a target for the number of prototypes entering the selection funnel;
- a target for the number of ideas generated by the staff;
- how long it takes for new products to go from idea approval to launch.

Phase VI: Questioning exercises

The questioning exercises are used to develop the participants' questioning skills and checking of assumptions. The recommended exercises from Appendix 1 are:

Exercise N – Lateral thinking puzzles.

Exercise R – Remote architects.

An hour spent on questioning techniques is a good investment at this stage, before the team returns to the business-specific issues.

Phase VII: Communications plan

Communication of the vision and its components, and of the strategic plan, is so important that it is worth spending a section of the workshop on this topic. The challenges to be addressed depend on where the organization is in its development and communication. These are the sorts of topics that should be considered:

- How can we communicate the vision, the mission, culture, values and purpose to the internal audience? Which of these messages should we prioritize?
- How can we communicate the vision to the external audience?
- How can we get the staff to buy into the vision?
- How can we develop departmental and personal objectives in line with our strategic goals?
- How can we communicate the need for creativity, innovation, ideas and entrepreneurial spirit?
- What mechanisms, training or processes can we put in place to generate a flow of ideas from all the staff?

The exercises that can be used here include Brainstorming, Break the rules, Similes and Random word. This should lead to a list of actions to improve communication, ranging from the mundane to the truly radical.

Phase VIII: Staff issues and empowerment

This section of the workshop addresses issues surrounding staffing, empowerment and human resource policies. The types of issues that are tackled include:

- What do we really want our people to be and to achieve?
- How can we recruit people who are creative and entrepreneurial?
- Are our people truly empowered today? If not, what can we do to empower them?
- What training and development do people need to fulfil our mutual ambitions?
- How can we inspire and motivate our staff to do the extraordinary?

To explore these topics, the facilitator uses exercises such as Brainstorming, Pass the parcel, Successive integration, Break the rules and Six serving men. The outcome from this phase should be a list of ideas, actions and proposals to improve staff motivation, training and empowerment.

Phase IX: Competitive and product workshop

If previous phases have overrun and fatigue is setting in, it is best to go straight to the summary and action list. However, if time allows and energy levels are still high, this is an excellent section to include at this stage. A good exercise to use is the Ideal competitor (Appendix 1, Exercise O). Divide into two teams and have each construct an ideal competitor that would use radical means to take a leadership position in the market. Each team presents its results, and a lively discussion should ensue. The question which the facilitator asks is, 'If a competitor can do these radical things, why can't we?'

Another fine exercise is Roll the dice (Appendix 1, Exercise K), which forces original combinations of product options and markets. It gets the team to think in terms of how they would market products that they would never normally consider.

Phase X: Innovation process and gating plan

Lateral leadership is all about inspiring people to be more creative, innovative and entrepreneurial. As part of the workshop the team reviews the processes in place in the organization to encourage and implement innovation. The innovation goals and metrics that we defined in an earlier phase are important inputs here. In particular, the team considers:

- How do we initiate the ideas process?
- How do we combine, adapt or modify ideas?
- In what areas do we need input from outside the organization?
- How will we choose which ideas to prototype?
- What gating process will we use to sift the prototypes?
- How will we roll out the successful prototypes into full production?
- How will we develop innovative business processes and procedures?
- How will we ensure a flow of innovative partnerships?

Exercises such as Brainstorming, Break the rules and The path to the ideal can be used. The outcome should be a systematic process to ensure that innovation happens throughout the company, from all departments, and from idea generation all the way through to finished innovation.

Phase XI: Summary and action list

The end of the final day is the time to pull together a summary of what has been agreed on in the workshop. The facilitator has been working behind the scenes to record all the ideas and annotate the ones that were agreed to be the most promising. The facilitator now helps the team pull together the following:

- The agreed vision, mission, culture and values statements.
- The strategic objectives and innovation goals and metrics.

- Lists of 'no-brainers' – easy things to implement which were agreed to be beneficial and which can be undertaken immediately.

- A list of ideas that are very promising but require further work and development. These should be delegated to individuals to investigate and progress.

- A list of wacky but possibly brilliant ideas which should be left to incubate for a while and then reconsidered at a later date.

- A defined innovation process.

- A feedback form on the workshop so that the team and facilitator can see what worked well and what did not for future reference.

Phase XII: Follow-up session

Two to three weeks later is the time to have a follow-up session at which the summary and action lists from the workshop are reviewed by the team. The 'no-brainers' should all be in place so their immediate impact can be reviewed. Early feedback on the vision can be assessed. There should be reports on some of the promising ideas. These can be reviewed and decisions taken. The innovation process should be in place so it can be used. The list of wacky ideas can be fed into the innovation process, and members of the senior team should join the innovation workshops from time to time to show willing and signal the importance of the process.

Also at the follow-up session there should be an honest review of whether there is real progress towards lateral leadership in the organization. Changing the corporate culture is a long and arduous process with many setbacks, so it is important to see the workshop as an early stage in a long journey. Staff training is needed at all levels. The new processes have to be developed, improved and made to work. The senior team needs constantly to review and renew its commitment to innovation. The organization needs to develop a restless quest for creativity, improvement and self-renewal at all levels.

APPENDIX 1
Tools and techniques

A Brainstorming

The most popular group creativity exercise in business is the brainstorm. It is quick, easy and it works. There are variations and enhancements to make it more powerful. But many organizations become frustrated with brainstorms and have stopped using them. They say they are old-fashioned and not so effective. The real reason for the frustrations is that the brainstorms are not run properly. Here are some simple rules to make sure that your brainstorm works well.

Set clear objectives

The purpose of the brainstorm is to generate many creative ideas to answer a specific goal. It is best to express the goal as a question. A vague or woolly question is not helpful. 'How can we increase sales?' is not as good as 'How can we double sales in the next 12 months?' However, the parameters of the questions should not be too detailed or it can close out lateral possibilities. 'How can we double sales, through existing channels and with the current product set?' is probably too constrained. Once the question has been agreed, it is written clearly for all to see.

It is worth setting objectives for the number of ideas to be generated and the time to be spent. 'We are looking to generate 60 ideas in the next 20 minutes. Then we will whittle them down to four or five really good ones.' The brainstorm should not be too long – between 30 and 45 minutes is generally best. The best size of group is somewhere between 6 and 12. Too few people and there are not enough diverse inputs. Too many people and it is hard to control the meeting and to retain everyone's commitment.

Suspend judgement

In order to encourage a wealth of wacky ideas it is essential that no one is critical, negative or judgemental about an idea. Any idea that is uttered – no matter how stupid – must be written down. The rule about suspending judgement during the idea generation phase is so important that it is worth enforcing rigorously. A good technique is to issue water pistols; anyone who is critical gets squirted.

Quantity is good

The more ideas the better. Brainstorming is one the few activities in life where quantity improves quality. Think of it as a Darwinian process. The more separate ideas that are generated, the greater the chance that some will be fit enough to survive. You need stacks of energy and buzz driving lots of wacky ideas. Crazy thoughts that are completely unworkable are often the springboards for other ideas that can be adapted into great new solutions. So keep the crazy ideas coming – you have to kiss a lot of frogs to find one prince!

Number and display

Number each idea. This makes it easier to cross-reference the ideas and to set goals. 'We've come up with 65 ideas – let's see if we can get to 80.' Each idea should be written down as a short action statement in just a few words. The ideas must be clearly visible to all partici-pants. Flip charts work well for this purpose. As each page is filled it is posted on the wall of the room so that the whole catalogue of ideas can be seen. When it comes time to analyse the ideas, all those that are linked can be circled in the same colour.

Analyse and select

The final step in the brainstorm session is to analyse the ideas. One of the best ways is to quickly go through them and perform a triage. Divide the proposals into a) promising, b) interesting possibility and c) reject. For example, you can quickly mark each a) with two ticks, each b) with one tick, and cross through the rejects. This is a group activity led by the moderator, and there is usually good consensus on what to do with most of the ideas. Any that are disputed can be put into category b). If time permits it is a good idea to then categorize and collect the ideas. If time is short do not worry; some people find that it is best to let the ideas stew for a while before returning to them at a later time when the subconscious has had the opportunity to turn them over. Either way, write on a separate flipchart all the ideas in categories a) and b) that are marketing ideas, say, and on another chart all the sales ideas, and so on. This process of rearranging the ideas can help you see new combinations and possibilities. You may well then find that you can synthesize ideas by putting together an a) with a b) to come up with a real winner. For further detailed analysis, a technique like six thinking hats (see S below) can be used.

An alternative method of selecting the best ideas is to give everyone 10 points that they can allocate to their favourite ideas in any way that they want. They can give one point to 10 separate ideas or all 10 to one idea. Then you total the points.

B Random word

As a stimulus to a brainstorm a random word, image or object can work wonders. Just pick up a dictionary and choose a noun at random. Then force connections between that word and the problem to be solved. You will find that all sorts of new associations spring to mind. Say the problem is how to get more people to use buses. The random word from the dictionary is – shark. Some of the ideas it triggers are:

- Free trips to the aquarium as lottery prizes using bus tickets as entries.
- Preferential loans for bus passengers (not at loan shark rates).
- Hot soup on buses in winter (shark's fin could be one variety).
- Music on buses to make the trip more pleasant (triggered by the Sharks and Jets in *West Side Story*).

Why does the random word work? It forces the brain to start from a new departure point, to come at the problem from a new direction. The brain is a lazy organ; it will automatically lapse into familiar patterns and solve problems the way it has always done unless you give it a jog and start it from a new point.

C Restate the problem

Restate the question in many different ways before trying to come up with solutions. Looking at the problem in a different light can often lead to insightful solutions straight off. The problem is written on a board in front of the group. Everyone then has to write down a different statement of the problem using none of the words used in the initial statement. So 'How can we increase sales?' could be expressed as 'What actions could lead to more revenue?' or 'Why shouldn't the company get more money from customers?' Everyone's restatements of the problem are written out and the different perspectives are used as triggers in the brainstorm session.

D Similes

A fruitful technique is to get everyone to write down on their own sheet of paper, 'Our problem is like…' and then to complete the sentence. The likenesses do not have to be accurate – they are feelings rather than exact analogies, but each can act as a trigger. For example, say the problem is, 'How can we increase customer order values?' Here are some of the responses you might get to 'Our problem is like…'

- '… getting a child to eat their meals.'
- '… filling a shopping trolley at the supermarket.'
- '… skiing uphill.'
- '… getting our football team to score more goals.'
- '… getting more done each day.'
- '… getting more apples from our apple tree.'

Each of these analogies draws on different personal experiences, and each can serve as a starting point for a productive brainstorm.

E Reverse the problem

State the issue in reverse then brainstorm. Say the question is, 'How can we reduce customer complaints?' Then it is restated as 'How can we increase customer complaints?' Initially the brainstorm ideas will be obviously customer-hostile ideas, but as you carry on you will probably identify things that to some extent are already happening in the organization. Once you have a good long list of all the things that can increase customer complaints, you go through them again looking at how you could reverse them in order to reduce complaints.

F Break the rules

List all the basic rules that apply in your organization or business environment and then deliberately break them. You then use the broken rules as springboards for new ideas. Say for example you were looking for ways to improve the productivity of your telemarketing department. Here are some of the rules that you might list as applying to the business today:

1 We use the telephone.

2 We call between 9 am and 12 noon, and 2 pm and 5 pm.

3 We are always polite and professional.

4 We use a script which has been carefully developed to deliver the right messages.

5 We reward our agents for the number of leads they generate.

6 We follow up each appointment with a confirmation letter and information pack.

Now we break the rules:

1 We will use other methods of contacting people than the telephone.

2 We will contact people outside normal business hours, such as early in the morning, at lunch time or in the evening.

3 We will be rude and unprofessional.

4 We will let our agents say whatever they want.

5 We will fine our agents for every lead they get.

6 We will not send out a confirmation by post.

How can any of these ideas help us to make the department more effective? Items 1 to 3 might suggest that we find creative ways to approach our target prospects as they arrive at or leave work. The telemarketing team could dress up as clowns and approach commuters getting off trains with humorous and outrageous messages which solicit responses. Item 4 might prompt us to think of ways in which we could make our message more interesting and less mechanical. The idea of fines might prompt us to emphasize to potential customers the costs and penalties of not responding. Finally, item 6 might lead to the ideas of confirming appointments through a special website or hand delivering to customers a package containing an attractive wall calendar with the date and time of our appointment highlighted.

G The worst solution

A variation on Reverse the problem is to try to conceive the worst solution to the original question. The brainstorm continues as normal, but everyone is trying to think of lousy ideas that definitely would not work or would make the problem worse. This can generate a lot of humorous energy in the group as they heap one bad idea on top of another. But when these atrocious ideas are subsequently analysed, some of them can be reversed to generate good ideas that represent novel solutions to the problem.

H Idea cards

The problem is stated and then every member of the group has to take two cards and write an idea in no more than four or five words on each card. The cards are shuffled and dealt out so that everyone has two cards. Ideally this should be done in such a way that they do not get back either of their own cards, and the two cards they receive are from different people. All the members then have to combine the two ideas before them into a new idea that they present to the group. After you have done this exercise once, try it again, but this time the members get three cards, on each of which they write one word only. The cards are shuffled, and everyone gets three cards with which to construct a proposition.

I Found objects

A technique recommended by Brian Clegg and Paul Birch in *Instant Creativity*, a good resource for trainers, is called 'Found objects' (Clegg and Birch, 1999: 53). At a natural break in proceedings (say lunch or a coffee break) everyone is instructed to bring back a random object after the break, but not told why. When they return with their objects after the break they are each given two challenges. They have to stand up and say with emotion and passion why their object is extremely interesting and how it will help solve the stated problem. Since the objects are often random, mundane items like paper clips or hairdryers, the challenge of speaking with passion will often be funny. But as people listen, they too have the challenge of trying to force associations between the object and the problem, and therefore coming up with new ideas. This exercise can add humour, energy and a good helping of fresh solutions.

J Pass the parcel

Pass the parcel is suitable for groups with a minimum of four and maximum of eight people. It forces people to come at problems from new directions and to think creatively. It works like this. Each person takes a blank sheet of paper and writes the challenge at the top. Then, working silently and individually, each person writes a completely crazy, bizarre and impossible solution to the question. No reasonable ideas are allowed at this stage; they have to be ridicu-lous. All the players then pass their sheet of paper to the person on their left. Now everyone has to use the idea in front of them as a springboard for another crazy idea. It can be based on the first, or different, but it should be triggered by the first idea. The sheets are then passed silently again to the left. All players now have a piece of paper in front of them with two crazy ideas. They have to use these to construct an outlandish but workable idea – one that is outrageous but feasible given enough resources. The sheets are passed again, and now the players have to use the three ideas before them as triggers to construct a novel but workable idea; one they could propose to their peers. All individuals in turn read out the four ideas on their sheet – usually to peals of laughter. The group then analyses all the final ideas and chooses one or two – or synthesizes some of the ideas to come up with a proposal.

For example, the challenge was, 'How can the village flower shop double its sales?' Here were four ideas as written in sequence on one sheet:

1 Get Tom Cruise to deliver each bouquet personally to the lady concerned.

2 Get Tom Cruise and Taylor Swift to deliver each bouquet and sing a duet on the doorstep.

3 Offer a night out at a romantic Broadway musical with every bouquet sold.

4 Partner with a record company to offer a CD of romantic love songs with bouquets at an attractive promotional price.

This exercise is good fun and often generates imaginative ideas. It involves silent individual action followed by group hilarity and discussion. It therefore makes a good change from the exercises that involve the whole group together all the time.

K Roll the dice

Roll the dice works well with groups of 4 to 10 people, and is excellent for forcing unusual combinations for new products or services. It is good to divide into two competing teams in separate rooms. All the equipment needed is a flipchart and a dice.

Table A1.1

Target	Medium	Promotion	Partner with
1 Mothers	Newspaper	Radio commercials	Local hospital
2 Cyclists	Magazine	Direct mail	Local schools
3 Anglers	Website	E-mail promotions	Major television station
4 Computer nerds	TV programme	Billboard advertising	Football club
5 Wealthy retired	E-mail newsletter	Telephone calling	Record company
6 Foreign visitors	Mailed subscription	Phone text messages	Fast food chain

You select three or four characteristics of the challenge and define six choices for each. For example, say you wanted to create a new publication. You might use the parameters shown in Table A1.1.

You then roll the dice four times. Let's say you roll 4, 4, 2, 6. The team has to conceive and design a plan for a television programme aimed at computer enthusiasts, promoted by direct mail and sponsored by or partnered with a fast food chain. They get 10 minutes to put together their plan and present it to the other team and the moderator. It is quite remarkable how combinations that initially look very unattractive can be moulded into interesting business propositions.

L Successive integration

Successive integration is a method developed at the Batelle Institute in Frankfurt. The problem is stated and then each member of the group silently writes down an idea relating to the problem. Two members of the group then read out their ideas. The others then combine the two ideas into one. A third person reads out his or her idea, and the group finds a way to integrate this new idea with the one formed from the first two. And so it goes on. The group tries to integrate each new idea into a synthesized solution. The method is systematic, every idea is explored, and novel combinations are forced.

M The path to the ideal

Set up three flipcharts. On the first, state the current state of affairs with all its flaws, problems and difficulties. On the third sheet, write the ideal state you would like to achieve with all problems solved and the organization performing superbly (or however you define ideal). Then on the top of the middle sheet write, 'The path.' Here you have to define the steps you need to take to get from where you are today to the ideal. This is not as creative as some of the other exercises, and it is unlikely to generate wild and innovative ideas, but it certainly helps to define the problem, and each of the steps on the path could themselves become questions that you can address using creative techniques.

N Lateral thinking puzzles

These are puzzles that develop questioning and imagination skills. The team has to work out the answer to a strange situation. The puzzles work well with groups of 5 to 10 people. They can be played as team games with different teams competing, provided the same questions are used and the moderators apply the same rules.

The moderator reads out the puzzle. People fire questions. The moderator (who knows the answer) can answer 'Yes', 'No' or 'Irrelevant' to each question. The participants learn that they need to ask many questions, and when they get stuck they have to come at the problem from a fresh direction. After 30 minutes the team that has solved the most puzzles is the winner.

An example puzzle is, 'A woman died because she bought some new shoes. How?' Obviously there could be many different explanations, but it is only through exhaustive questioning and trying new approaches that the answer is found. She was the assistant of a blindfolded knife thrower in a circus. Her heels were higher and this produced the fatal result.

People often start slowly and then speed up as they get the idea. It is a different kind of creative exercise. Many lines are explored in order to narrow down to one. The participants are trying to find the given solution rather than any creative solution. The puzzles are excellent training in questioning, in imagination, and in coming at a problem from different directions.

O The ideal competitor

This is a good exercise for two or more teams of about four to six people each. The brief is simple. Imagine that an immensely wealthy corporation has decided to enter your business market and plans to create a powerful competitor which will use innovative approaches to seize your current organization's customers and wipe you out. It will deliberately exploit your weaknesses to hurt you in the marketplace. This corporation has hired your team to put together the new competitor, and given you immense resources. What would you do?

Each team has to brainstorm innovative ways of reaching the customer, delivering better services and seizing a leading market share. The teams present their ideas and the moderator decides on a winner. The emphasis is placed on creative ideas rather than undercutting on price or outspending on promotions. Obviously many of the ideas generated are ones that your organization should be investigating urgently before a real 'ideal competitor' emerges.

P What if?

In the What if? exercise every dimension of the question is tested with 'what if...?' questions. The more ridiculous the questions the better. Say the question is, 'In order to reduce congestion, how can we persuade people to use their cars less and public transport more?' The sort of 'what if?' questions we could ask might be:

- What if congestion was 10 times worse than it is now?
- What if no one was allowed to drive a car?
- What if public transport was free?

- What if public transport collected you from your door and delivered you to your destination?
- What if people could fly?
- What if we prevented all road accidents, injuries and deaths?
- What if the maximum speed limit was 10 mph?
- What if the maximum speed limit was 1,000 mph?
- What if there was a minimum speed limit?
- What if this problem applied to air transport and the skies were congested with private planes?
- What if it cost US $1 million a year to own a car?
- What if we had unlimited funds to make public transport more attractive?
- What if this problem had applied in ancient Rome to chariots?
- What if people were forced to live within five miles of their place of work?
- What if we doubled the number or width of roads?

Each question prompts ideas, and tests the rules and boundaries that are assumed to apply to the problem.

Q Six serving men

This exercise examines an issue from 12 views, based on the words of the poem by Rudyard Kipling:

I keep six honest serving men

They taught me all I knew

Their names are What and Why and When

And How and Where and Who.

We probe the topic using these questioning words from a positive and negative perspective. The issue is defined as a question, then 12 sheets of flipchart paper are arranged around the room. On each sheet one of the 12 questions is written as the heading, and the team then comes up with answers to that question. Suppose the issue is, 'How can we improve customer service in our retail centres?' The questions could be constructed as follows:

1 What is good customer service?

2 What is not good customer service?

    (Or what is bad customer service?)

3 Why do we get good customer service?

4 Why do we get bad customer service?

5 When is there good customer service?

6 When is there bad customer service?

7 How do we get good customer service?

8 How do we get bad customer service?

9 Where is there good customer service?

10 Where is there bad customer service?

11 Who gives good customer service?

12 Who gives bad customer service?

By repeatedly approaching the questions of good service and bad service, and by forcing people to come up with new answers and inputs, the exercise paints a broad picture of the issue and the underlying factors. The ideas on the sheets are analysed and combined to come up with potential proposals to address the issue.

R Remote architects

This is a good game for developing a more precise questioning technique. The participants are divided into pairs. One person in each pair is given a picture of a house (see the sample pictures, Figures A1.1 and A1.2, which can be used for this exercise). The second person in the pair does not see the picture but has to ask questions about the house and draw an image of it based on the answers to the questions.

Figure A1.1

SOURCE Monika Schröder, Pixabay

Figure A1.2

SOURCE Dani Myrick, Pixabay

The responder must give precise answers to the questions asked but not volunteer information and should not see or comment on the image as it is drawn. After five minutes of questioning and drawing the picture that has been drawn is compared to the picture of the house and the pair talk about the communication process. The pair then switch roles and repeat the exercise using a different picture of a house.

In the normal game the questioner can ask questions that are either open-ended (eg 'Describe the roof to me') or closed (eg 'Is the door at the centre of the front?') The game can be altered by the use of variants in the rules, such as that the questioner may ask only two open-ended questions, and the rest must be closed questions, or the questioner may only ask closed questions.

The game is a clever exercise in questioning. It teaches the importance of asking the right questions and checking assumptions. It shows the value of open-ended questions to begin with in order to get the overall impression, and closed questions to determine precise details.

S Six thinking hats

Six thinking hats is an excellent proposal analysis tool created by Edward de Bono (1985). It can be used in many situations ranging from council meetings to jury rooms. It is particularly useful for evaluating innovative and provocative ideas.

As de Bono points out, most of our thinking is adversarial. You put up an idea and I criticize it in order to test the strength of the idea. Prosecution and defence in a courtroom, or government and opposition parties in Parliament are good examples of adversarial thinking. The trouble is that adversarial thinking in business meetings can be entrenched and politicized. For example, the sales manager opposes an idea because it came from the marketing manager. Both parties then dig in to reinforce their positions. Also, people can be inhibited from criticizing ideas their boss puts forward.

The six thinking hats technique overcomes these difficulties by forcing everyone to think in parallel. As they wear each hat they all have to think a certain way at the same time. Here is how it works. The proposal is read out and then everyone puts on the following hats in turn:

1 **The white hat.** This is the information hat, and people can ask for more information or data to help analyse the proposal.

2 **The red hat.** This hat represents emotions. People have to say how this proposal makes them feel emotionally. For example, some might say they feel threatened or scared by this idea. Others might say they feel excited. It is important to get the feelings expressed, as they can be hidden reasons why people would oppose or support a proposal.

3 **The yellow hat.** This hat is the optimism hat. Everyone in turn has to say what is good about the proposal. Even if you think the idea stinks you have to find some redeeming qualities and good points about it.

4 **The black hat** is the hat of pessimism. Everyone has to find fault with the idea. Even if it was your idea and you are very proud of it you have to point out some drawbacks and disadvantages.

5 **The green hat** is the hat of growth and possibilities. Everyone has to suggest ways in which the idea could be adapted or improved to make it work better.

6 **The blue hat** is the process hat that is used to check if the process is working well. When you wear it, you discuss whether you are using the method in the most effective way.

Generally you will spend fairly little time with the blue hat, a little more with the white and red hats, but most time with the yellow, black and green hats. You can go back and forth from one hat to another, but the key rule is that everyone must wear the same hat at the same time. It is good to have a chairperson who holds up a coloured card or turns over a coloured cube to show which hat is in use and to make sure everyone is on board. If the chairperson sees someone using black hat thinking during the yellow hat session, that person must be brought back into line.

The method is simple to run, and remarkably effective in quickly and productively analysing proposals. If you want to use this method, de Bono's book on the subject, *Six Thinking Hats* (1985) is highly recommended.

T Rapid-fire storytelling

In this creativity exercise, team members take turns to add one line of a story. This should be done at pace and with no criticism or judgement of previous contributions. The story can dart into all manner of crazy directions, but each contributor should build on what has gone before.

An example might start something like this:

A mad scientist called Terry was working in his laboratory late at night.

Suddenly the window blew open and a bolt of lightning struck the table.

Chemicals and ingredients were blasted everywhere.

The next morning his assistant found Terry burnt and dazed.

His hair had turned blue.

There was a strange whining noise in the background.

Suddenly Terry leapt up.

'At last I have the answer,' he shouted.

This is a good icebreaker with a team who need to be shaken out of their regular business thought processes and into a more creative and relaxed mode. It should be fun and is a good energizer to get a workshop going or to liven things up after lunch. Typically it will have served its purpose after two or three stories have been developed.

U Spending £10

This is an evaluation exercise to be used when you have generated a number of good ideas and want to focus quickly on the most promising. Each member of the team is given a notional £10 (or $10 or other currency) to allocate on his or her favourite ideas. People can allocate £1 to each of 10 ideas, £10 to one idea, or any mixture in between, but they cannot allocate fractions of pounds. They work separately and in silence for a few minutes to choose their selections. The funds are then allocated and totalled. The projects with the most money attached are taken forward.

V What's on television tonight?

In this creativity exercise the challenge or issue is defined, then a television guide is found with tonight's programmes listed. The challenge is then seen through the eyes of the characters in the television programmes, and their responses or solutions are imagined and discussed. Say the challenge is how to attract more visitors to an art gallery, and the programmes that evening include:

- *Game of Thrones*;
- celebrity dancing (*Strictly Come Dancing* or *Dancing with the Stars*);
- a wildlife programme on sharks;
- an interview with Lady Gaga.

The team would first discuss how the characters in *Game of Thrones* would tackle such a challenge, and drop into the roles and personas of the different players. Many macho, warlike and fantasy ideas to make the art gallery attractive might be suggested. Then the team would imagine how the dancing stars and judges would approach the issue each in their different styles. Then the point of view of a naturalist or even a shark would be employed. Finally the team would try to think how Lady Gaga would see the issue, and what solutions she might propose.

The purpose is to explore different approaches by forcing the team to adopt the characteristics of familiar television shows from different genres. A good mix of serious and humorous programmes, soaps and documentaries will help fire different ideas and proposals.

W Scamper

Scamper is a good method for generating ideas for new products. It was originally conceived by the marketing legend Alex Osborn, who is also credited with the concept of brainstorms. It involves looking at the product from seven specific viewpoints and asking the appropriate question at each juncture:

1 **Substitute.** Can we substitute anything for or in the product?

2 **Combine.** Can we combine the product with something?

3 **Adapt.** How can we adapt the product for the customer?

4 **Magnify/minify.** How can we magnify the product or minimize it?

5 **Put to other use.** How can we put the product to another use?

6 **Eliminate.** How can we eliminate some aspect of the product?

7 **Rearrange/reverse.** What happens if we rearrange or reverse the product or service?

By asking these questions in a systematic way and by being uninhibited in our initial answers we can stretch our view of the product into entirely different possibilities.

X Transformers

Transformers is a variant of the Scamper method. It is a particularly good method if you are looking to improve or radically change a process. Take the problem and draw it as a simple flow process. Then take verbs at random from a list of 'transformer verbs'. Here are some of the verbs you can use:

Add	Help	Reinforce	Stretch
Bypass	Integrate	Reverse	Submerge
Distort	Invert	Rotate	Substitute
Divide	Magnify	Segregate	Subtract
Eliminate	Minimize	Separate	Symbolize
Extract	Multiply	Soften	Transpose
Flatten	Protect	Squeeze	Unify
Freeze	Rearrange		

Say that you are seeking to improve your sales process for selling flowers and you are assigned the verb 'rearrange'. Then you would deliberately make extreme rearrangements. What if we delivered the flowers before the customer had ordered them? We could do that by taking annual orders years in advance, for example for anniversaries. What if we rearranged the flower shop so that customer called in his order and we delivered at the railway station? And so on. It is important to use the verbs in very intense ways in order to disturb and stimulate the process.

Y Personalities

The challenge is stated and then a personality is chosen at random from a list that includes many well-known, outspoken or controversial people. Some of the person's traits and characteristics are listed and then the question is asked, 'How would this person approach the problem?' Drawing on what is known of the personality, people suggest ways in which the chosen individual would tackle the issue. It is best to take their approach to extremes.

This is another idea-generation technique that displaces people from their normal line of attack and gives them licence to explore the issue from a different point of view.

A list of 60 personalities is available from the *Destination Innovation* website but by all means substitute other characters if you feel that they are better known or more provocative for your team.

You can choose an item at random from this list of 60 by simply glancing at the second hand of a watch or clock. The exact reading in seconds gives the number of the personality.

Z The ideas board

The challenge is written at the top of a sheet which is then put up at, say, the back of the room. During a certain period – it can be a day for a workshop or a week in the office – everyone has to add at least one new idea for solving the problem. People have to read the ideas that have already been posted and then add a new one of their own. The ideas can be added anonymously or attributed – whichever you prefer. The most obvious answers tend to be posted first so the later you join in the process the more creative you have to be. This method is good where you want people to dwell on the matter and then add a considered opinion.

APPENDIX 2
Answers to lateral thinking puzzles

The subway problem

The engineer changed the bulbs to have left-hand or anti-clockwise threads instead of the conventional right-hand or clockwise threads. This meant that as thieves assumed they were trying to unscrew the bulbs they were actually tightening them instead.

Vandal scandal

The authorities arranged for some chips of marble from the same original quarry source as the Parthenon to be distributed around the site each day. Tourists thought they had picked up a piece from the original columns and were satisfied. (From Sloane and MacHale, 1993.)

Shoe shop shuffle

The shoe shops put single shoes as display items outside the shops. One shop put out left shoes, the other three shops put out right shoes. Thieves stole the display shoes but had to make pairs, so more shoes were taken from the one displaying left shoes. The manager changed the display to right shoes and thefts dropped significantly. (From Sloane and MacHale, 1993.)

The school inspection

Before the superintendent arrived the teacher instructed the pupils always to raise their left hands if they did not know the answer or were unsure. If they were sure they knew the answer they should raise their right hand. The teacher chooses a different pupil every time, but always one who had raised his or her right hand. The superintendent was duly impressed. (From Sloane and MacHale, 1993.)

Brush fires

They bought or rented herds of goats and grazed them on the mountain slopes. The goats ate the vegetation, kept the brush down and reached steep slopes that were otherwise difficult to reach. Brushwood fires were significantly reduced.

The coconut millionaire

The man is a philanthropist who buys great quantities of coconuts to sell to poor people at prices they can afford. He started out as a billionaire but lost so much money in his good works that he became a millionaire. If you assumed that the only way to become a millionaire is by working your way up to that level of wealth, you made an assumption which prevented you from solving the problem! (From Sloane and MacHale, 1997.)

Wrong number

The marketing manager called the telephone company that issued numbers and bought the wrong number. The line was redirected to the call centre and the mailing was sent out.

Two cities

The two cities are veracity and duplicity. Did you assume they were real cities containing the words truth and lie?

The stockbroker

He started with a list of 800 wealthy people and sent half of them a forecast that IBM stock would rise in the next week and half of them a forecast that IBM would fall. IBM fell, so he chose the 400 who had received the correct prediction. He sent 200 a forecast that GE would rise and 200 a forecast that GE would fall in the next week. He carried on with this process until he had 25 people for whom he had made five consecutive correct forecasts. He approached each and persuaded several to move their stock portfolios to him.

The unusual

The answer is a hairdryer, a lawnmower and a jack. Why did you assume it was one thing? (What would happen if you combined these three into one?)

Price tag

The practice originated to ensure that the clerk had to open the till and give change for each transaction. This recorded the sale and prevented the clerk from pocketing the money. (From Sloane and MacHale, 1997.)

Lost in the desert

The two men were unknown to each other and started apart. Did you assume that they started walking from the same place?

The seven bells

It was originally a mistake but the shop owner found that so many people came into the shop to point out the error that it increased business. (From Sloane and MacHale, 1998.)

Interview question

Of the many candidates at the interview only one gave this answer, which was judged the best. You give the car keys to your old friend and ask them to drive the sick old lady to hospital, while you wait at the bus stop with the person of your dreams.

Single-handed

He keeps the receipt and goes back to the shop to change the lightbulb!

Material gains

He cut up the strong cotton material of his tents and used it to make trousers that he sold to the miners. The man's name was Levi Strauss. By adapting to market conditions and innovating he was able to create a brand that has lasted to this day.

Golden gate

The Golden Gate bridge is not flat; it has an arch. It was designed that way to provide for heavy loads. When the controllers have to bring a tall crane under the bridge they judge the tides and stop all traffic, causing the bridge to achieve its highest clearance. The bridge weighs 887,000 tons and has a clearance of 220 feet (depending on tide). (Contributed by Tim Dowd.)

Late train

The train was at 22.10 which the man misheard as 20 to 10. It just goes to show how you have to check your assumptions!

easyJet

The second benefit to easyJet from their policy of no free drinks is that they can eliminate one lavatory from their planes because of the lower demand. This makes way for extra seats. (From Salter, 2002: 100.)

REFERENCES AND RECOMMENDED READING

Allan, D, Kingdon, M, Murrin, K and Rudkin, D (1999) *What If!*, Capstone, Oxford

Amabile, T, Hadley, C and Kramer, S (2002) Creativity under the gun, *Harvard Business Review* (Aug), pp 52–61

Ames, C (1990) *Boardroom Reports* (15 Feb), p 2

Bhide, A (1999) *The Origin and Evolution of New Businesses*, Oxford University Press, Oxford

Buzan, T (1988) *Make the Most of Your Mind*, Pan, London

Buzan, T (1993) *The Mind Map Book*, BBC Publications, London

Byrne, J, (2002) After Enron: the ideal corporation, *Business Week* (26 Aug), pp 32–35

Charan, R and Useem, J (2002) Why companies fail, *Fortune* (27 May), pp 36–44

Chisholm, Sir J (2002) Lecture at the IEE, London (Oct)

Clegg, B and Birch, P (1999) *Instant Creativity*, Kogan Page, London

Cooper, R (2001) *Winning at New Products*, Perseus Books, New York

Cooper, R (2002) *Winning at New Products* [online] www.prod-dev.com [accessed April 2017]

Cooper, R and Edgett, S (2001) Optimizing the stage-gate process, *Research Technology Management* (Fall)

Covey, S (1989) *The Seven Habits of Highly Effective People*, Simon and Schuster, New York

Cox, G (2001) *Ready, Aim, Fire Problem-Solving*, Oak Tree Press, Cork

De Bono, E (1970) *Lateral Thinking*, Penguin, Harmondsworth

De Bono, E (1971) *Lateral Thinking for Management*, Penguin, Harmondsworth

De Bono, E (1985) *Six Thinking Hats*, Penguin, Harmondsworth

De Bono, E (1992) *Sur/Petition*, Harper Business, New York

Drucker, P (1985) *Innovation and Entrepreneurship*, Butterworth Heinemann, Oxford

EC (2001) *European Commission Innovation Paper No 22*, Innobarometer, European Commission, Brussels

Euromonitor (2002) Textile washing products, *Euromonitor International* (Jun)

Farson, R and Keyes, R (2002) The failure-tolerant leader, *Harvard Business Review*, (Aug), pp 64–71

Foster, J (1996) *How to Get Ideas*, Berret-Koehler, San Francisco

Fradette, M and Michaud, S (1998) *The Power of Corporate Kinetics*, Simon and Schuster, New York

Gladwell, M (2002) *The Tipping Point*, Abacus, London

Hall, D (1995) *Jump Start Your Brain*, Warner, New York

Handy, C (1994) *The Empty Raincoat*, Hutchinson, London

Harvey-Jones, J (1993) *Managing to Survive*, Heinemann, London

Jobs, S (1988) *The Journey Is the Reward*, Lynx Books, New York

Kaner, S (1996) *Facilitator's Guide to Participatory Decison-Making*, New Society Publishers, British Columbia

Kelley, T (2001) *The Art of Innovation*, Harper Collins, London

Kennedy, P (2016) *Inventology*, Bantam Press, London

Kriegel, R (1991) *If It Ain't Broke... Break It!*, Warner, New York

Mattimore, B (1994) *99% Inspiration*, Amacom, New York

Michalko, M (1998) *Cracking Creativity*, Ten Speed Press, Berkeley

Morgan, A (1999) *Eating the Big Fish*, Adweek Books, New York

Orridge, M (1996) *75 Ways to Liven Up Your Training*, Gower, Aldershot

Peters, T (1994) *The Tom Peters Seminar*, Vintage, New York

Product Development Institute (2002) Stage-Gate [online] www.prod-dev. com [accessed April 2017]

Reid, G (2002) Turbulence, flexibility and performance of the long-lived small firm, *The Times* (25 Jun), p 32

Ridderstrale, J and Nordstrom, K (1999) *Funky Business*, Bookhouse Publishing, Sweden

Robinson, K (2001) *Out of our Minds*, Capstone, Oxford

Salter, C (2002) Ivy Ross is not playing around, *Fast Company* (Nov), pp 104–10

Sethi R, Smith D and Whan Park, C (2002) How to kill a team's creativity, *Harvard Business Review* (Aug), pp 16–17

Sloane, P (1991) *Lateral Thinking Puzzlers*, Sterling, New York

Sloane, P (1994) *Test Your Lateral Thinking IQ*, Sterling, New York

Sloane, P (1999) Are you a lateral leader? *Innovative Leader*, 8 (8)

Sloane, P (2002) Ten great ways to crush creativity, *Business Age* (Oct)

Sloane, P and MacHale, D (1993) *Challenging Lateral Thinking Puzzles*, Sterling, New York

Sloane, P and MacHale, D (1997) *Perplexing Lateral Thinking Puzzles*, Sterling, New York

Sloane, P and MacHale, D (1998) *Ingenious Lateral Thinking Puzzles*, Sterling, New York

Sloane, P and MacHale, D (2000) *Super Lateral Thinking Puzzles*, Sterling, New York

Stein, N (2002) Deadline USA, *Fortune* (8 Jul), pp 67–70

Swatch (2002) Swatch Company History [online] http://www.swatch-group.ch/company/past.php [accessed April 2017]

Thornton, P and Follos, M (2002) *Strategy, Paradigms and Cowdung*, Peter Bowman Group

Tischler, L (2002) He struck gold on the Net, *Fast Company* (Jun) pp 40–44

Tucker, R (2002) *Driving Growth through Innovation*, Berrett-Joehler, California

von Oech, R (1983) *A Whack on the Side of the Head*, Warner, New York

Warner, F (2002a) How Google searches itself, *Fast Company* (July)

Warner, F (2002b) Detroit muscle, *Fast Company* (Jun), pp 88–94

Welch, J (2001) *Jack: What I've learned leading a great company and great people*, Headline, New York

Wolf, J (2001) *Do Something Different*, Virgin Books, London, pp 50–54

Wujec, T (1995) *Five Star Mind*, Doubleday, Toronto

INDEX

Note: page numbers in *italic* indicate figures or tables.

CPSIA information can be obtained
at www.ICGtesting.com
Printed in the USA
JSHW041112091220
10123JS00005B/91

9 780749 481025